FAMILY

in

WEST YORKSHIRE

Howard Beck

Scarthin Books, Cromford, Derbyshire 1991

**FAMILY WALKS
IN WEST YORKSHIRE**

Family Walks Series
General Editor: Norman Taylor

THE COUNTRY CODE

Enjoy the countryside and respect its life and work
Guard against all risk of fire
Fasten all gates
Keep your dogs under close control
Keep to public paths across farmland
Use gates and stiles to cross fences, hedges and walls
Leave livestock, crops and machinery alone
Take your litter home
Help to keep all water clean
Protect wildlife special care on country roads
Make no unnecessary noise

Published 1991

Phototypesetting, printing by Nuffield Press Ltd., Cowley, Oxford.

ISBN 0 907758 43 6

EASTERGATE BRIDGE (Route 2)

Preface

Many people have an unfounded concept of the Industrial North, particularly that part of Yorkshire known before the 1976 political boundary changes nonsense as the West Riding. Mile upon mile of dismal moors, rolling above grimy stone towns and Satanic mills like black storm clouds on a chill wind, is how some see it. However, it is anything but the gloomscape these Philistines would have the uninitiated believe.

The region enjoys a blend of landscape that is unique, dramatic at times and in which 7000 years of man's aspirations is etched irrevocably into the fabric of the region. Both the valleys and the wind-swept gritstone moorlands are coloured with the remains of mysterious Bronze Age cult sites, Celtic hill forts, Roman roads and place-names that owe allegiance to the Anglo-Saxon, Viking and Norman invaders down the centuries.

West Yorkshire offers walking country par excellence, every bit as attractive as that to be found in better known areas, but then I could be accused of bias, being born and bred in the county. So, dear reader, walk on and let the routes described in this book be your guide and judge for yourself. Pleasant walking!

About the author

Howard Beck works as a freelance photographer and writer of guides and books. His work has appeared in many local and national publications, including The Lady, Country Walking, Illustrated London News, The Field, Yorkshire Life, Police Journal and the Dalesman. Family Walks in Three Peaks and Malham is a companion volume in this series. Other books by the author include:

GAPING GILL, 150 years of Exploration (Hale).
BRONTË COUNTRY [joint photographer] (Trodd Pub.).
FAMILY WALKS AROUND SKIPTON (Dalesman).
WORDSWORTH COUNTRY (under consideration).
CAVES OF THE CLOUD FORESTS (in preparation).

CONTENTS

LOCATION MAP

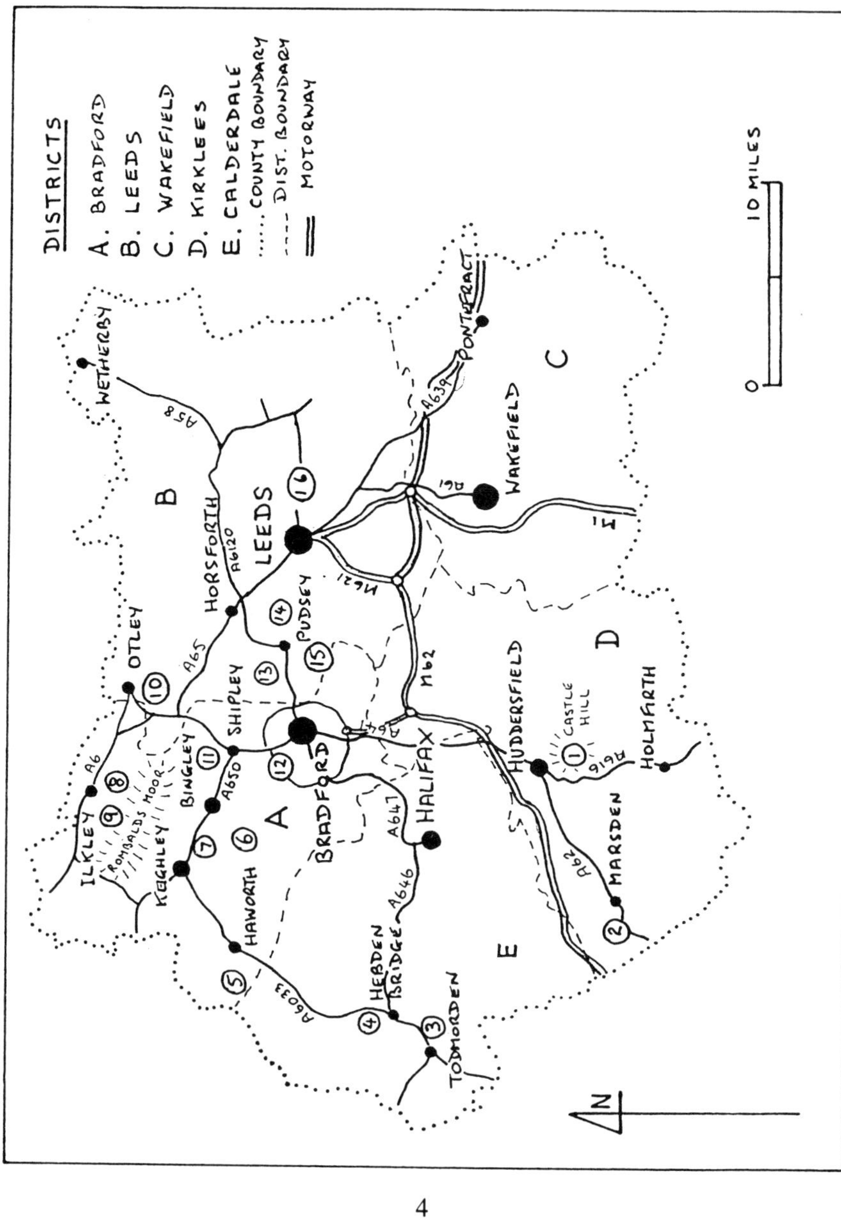

Introduction

This volume of walks is designed principally but not exclusively for the family group with children, and aims as with other books in this Series, to stimulate and excite the younger generation into appreciating the finer aspects of the countryside. It may come as a pleasant surprise to walkers more familiar with regions such as the Yorkshire Dales or North York Moors, to discover such a wide spectrum of unspoilt landscape so near to the county's major conurbations. All the routes are circular walks, where possible avoiding steep gradients and too much road walking. I have planned each outing to include features which will retain the interest of children, for instance waterfalls, woods, play areas, legends or strange stones.

Choosing a walk

Unless children in the party are seasoned ramblers it is perhaps advisable to select easier routes initially, moving on to more sustained expeditions at a later date. In the Appendix at the end of the book an attempt has been made to grade the walks in terms of difficulty. The reader may find this of value in choosing suitable walks that avoid placing too great a demand on younger children too soon. The aim is to nurture interest rather than to put the child off walking for life!

Allowing sufficient time

Many of the walks will form the best part of a day's outing, at a child's pace, allowing time off for play, exploration and rest stops, whilst for one or two a half day will suffice. It is infinitely better to over-estimate rather than under-estimate the time required; there is nothing worse than having to route march the last stages of the journey. As a rough guideline, allow a pace of around one mile per hour for very young children, graduating to two miles an hour for, say, the more experienced ten-year old.

What to wear

The British weather being what it is demands that walkers go prepared for the worst. Robust, but comfortable fell shoes or walking boots are more desirable than wellingtons, even though the latter have their place in English folk heritage! They do tend to chafe on long walks. Waterproof outer garments are an essential rather than a luxury, while underneath several layers of thin woollies are far better than one thick jumper. They tend to be warmer when the conditions are cold and in hotter weather (we do get it warm now and again) allow greater flexibility. A strong rucksack is essential for carrying spare clothing, food, drink, maps and so on. Don't forget a woolly hat and gloves.

Finding the way

Most of the walking described is along well defined and marked public footpaths, bridleways and green lanes, with the occasional stretch of road where this is unavoidable. Though each of the route descriptions and maps should be sufficiently detailed for navigation it is recommended that the relevant Ordnance Survey sheet is taken along as well. Should the reader find a path obstructed then the line of least resistance around it should be sought and the problem reported either to the Ramblers Association or to the relevant District Council.

Refreshments

Most of the pubs along these walks allow children on the premises if accompanied by an adult. Many cater for young children to the inclusion of play areas or special rooms. Bar meals and lunches are usually available but a good alternative, and one which will go down well with the younger walker, is to take along a picnic. Places on route where this is ideal are mentioned, as are the locations of cafes and tea shops.

Public transport

Although these days most families possess a car or other means of transport, I have included where this is relevant, details on bus operators, trains, etc., in the Appendices.

JUBILEE TOWER, CASTLE HILL

Symbols used on the route maps

Route 1 **4 miles**

Castle Hill

Outline Honley Station—Hey Wood—Lumb—Castle Hill—Honley Station.

Summary Field paths, woodland trails and green tracks take the walker through an area of rural charm at the heart of the Kirklees District. This is a walk with an easy beginning a more difficult middle and an easy finish. Without doubt the focus of attention is Castle Hill with its deep well and 100 feet high Jubilee Tower, a prominent landmark for miles around.

Attractions It's hard to imagine that, within 10 minutes of starting out from Honley railway station, urban sprawl will be left behind in favour of peaceful countryside. However a brief route through a residential area quickly gives way to a field path heading off uphill into pleasant broad leaf woodlands towards Farnley Bank. Once clear of the woods glimpses of Castle Hill can be seen over to the walker's left.

After level going through farmland and a short stretch of tarmac road, a green track and thin tree cover dives into a wooded dell beneath Lumb, above which Jubilee Tower bulks large in the view. A footbridge spans a small brook here, forming an ideal place for a picnic or a chance to play. Mum and Dad may care to take a breather here too for a stiff climb follows on the last pull up to Castle Hill.

Fortunately the climb does not go on for ever. The gradient eases after passing through Lumb, then around the back of a farm, ends abruptly at the windswept summit where the earthen ramparts of the fort are clearly seen. Despite its modest height of only 900 feet Castle Hill commands a wide prospect of West Yorkshire and the Pennines.

Since as early as Neolithic (late Stone Age) times there has been fortifications on Castle Hill. Apart from our Stone Age ancestors the Celts also established a hill fort here in 555 BC. Queen Cartimandua is believed to have led the Brigantes tribe from headquarters here during the Roman conquest. The magnificent prospect from the summit gave rise to the romantic notion that here King Arthur held his legendary court of Camelot.

The Normans in 1147 restored and strengthened the ancient earthworks, creating a motte and bailey fort. On the south side of the tower may be seen an 80 feet deep well dating from the 14th century. In more recent times Castle Hill has seen cock fighting, dog fighting and prize fighting. A beacon fire was lit as warning of the Spanish Armada, while the tower itself was opened in 1899 as a memorial to Queen Victoria's Diamond Jubilee.

continued on page 12

Route 1

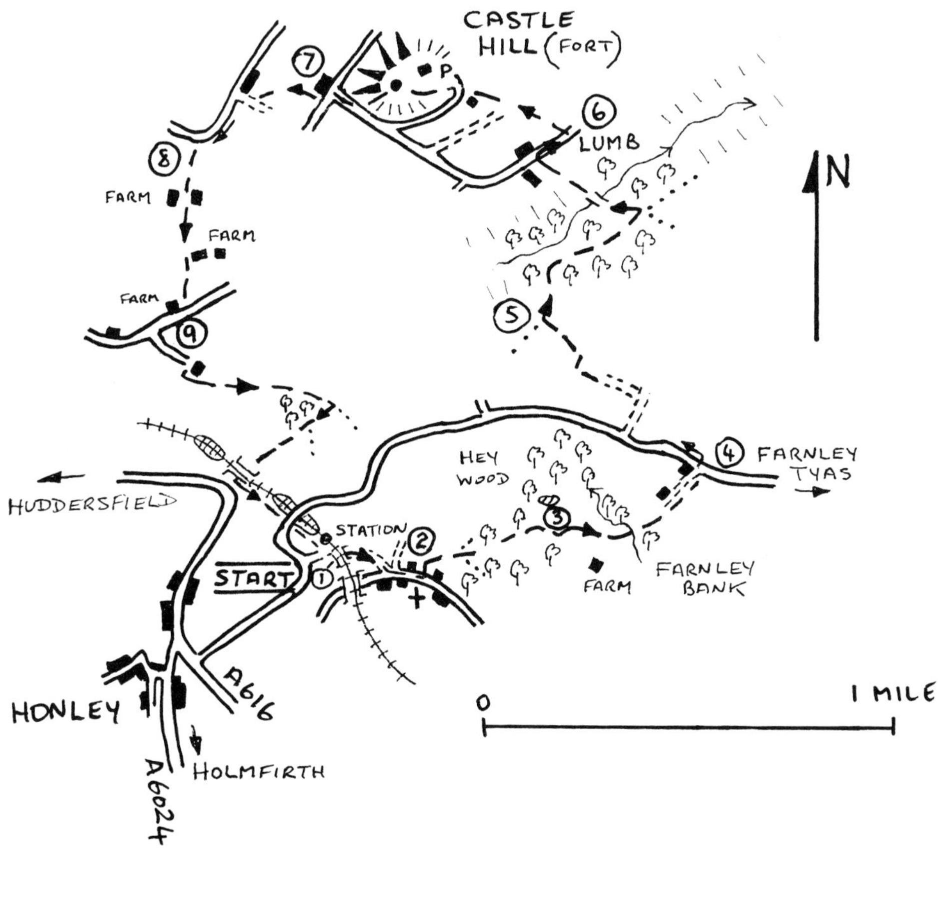
CASTLE
HILL (FORT)
P
7
6
LUMB
N
8
FARM
FARM
FARM
5
9
HEY
WOOD
4
FARNLEY
TYAS
HUDDERSFIELD
STATION
2
3
START
1
FARNLEY
BANK
FARM
HONLEY
A616
0
1 MILE
HOLMFIRTH
A6024

Route 1

Castle Hill — 4 miles

START: *At Honley railway station located just off the A616 Sheffield road 4 miles south of Huddersfield. Park in the road just outside the station. (G.R. SE146124) O.S. Landranger sheet 110 (Sheffield and Huddersfield).*

ROUTE

1. *With the station building on your left walk through the tunnel under the line to reach a gate. Go through this and turn right along a pathway between houses leading onto a dirt road. Walk down this to a junction, then turn left along Hall Ing Lane. Walk up this as far as Woodroyd Chapel on your right.*
2. *Opposite this turn left along a path between gardens to a stile. Go through this and with a power line pole on your left make a beeline for the woods 50 yards ahead. Pass through a gap in the wall and, ignoring paths left and right, walk forward on the well defined middle path uphill through Hey Wood. Ignore a track cutting across the route part way up the hill.*
3. *At the top of the wood turn left along the wall side to a gap stile. Ignore the path going right here to continue forward around the rim of the ravine, then with a wall now on your left a stream is forded at a wall corner 120 yards ahead. Climb the steps, cross a stile and turn left. Walk beside the wall keeping a farm on your left, passing through a gate, then a stile. Continue with the wall on your left to reach a tarmac road via another stile.*
4. *Beyond the stile turn left down the road then turn right along the first green lane. When this ends walk along the left edge of the field to a gate. Go through this and turn right to a wall corner. From here cut across a field to a stile in the far right hand corner by a row of holly trees. Go through the stile and cross a farm track to follow continuing path to some power line poles and a stile on your right.*
5. *Go through the stile and walk along a holly hedge to a stile. Turn left through this and follow right edge of field to cross a stile by a stream. Turn right. Walk parallel with the stream and go through a gap in a fence. 250 yards further on bear left to a fence and follow this right to a stile. Go through this, descending to a footbridge and climb the banking to a stile. Follow the obvious field path ascending to Lumb.*

6. *Go through a stile at top of the field, turn right down a lane, then left at the next stile. Still climbing, a clear path is traced behind a farm to where the path meets a tarmac road at the summit of Castle Hill. Descend the steps on the opposite side of the tower to the pub to return to the lane. Turn right to reach a road junction.*
7. *Cross Ashes Lane and go through a stile to the left of a cottage. Walk down by a hedgerow and cross a stile, then head for the bottom left corner of the next field to reach a track. Turn right along this, then left at Bower Lane.*
8. *At an acute right bend walk forward along a track to a gate at a farm. Go through this and follow the track to the left, at the next gate turning right. Walk forward and to the left around a barn to reach a wall corner. Go through the stile here and head uphill to a gate left of the next farm. Turn right through a gate and walk down the lane to a driveway on the left.*
9. *Turn along this but just before house take the path to your right alongside the garden and pass through a hedge. Turn left and following field path, eventually passing along the top side of a wood to a stile. Go through this down some steps to a gate and stile. Cross this then turn right down through gorse bushes to a stile 60 yards below. Continue downhill to the railway embankment. Climb a stile and go through the tunnel, turning immediately left up a flight of steps. Follow a path between houses and the railway, crossing the Farnley Tyas road and continuing back to Honley Station.*

ACCESS BY BUS
Bus services from Huddersfield.

Upon leaving Castle Hill field paths lead through farmland flanking the Holme Valley, before passing beneath the Sheffield to Bradford rail line and following this back to Honley station.

Refreshments The Castle pub adjacent to the tower welcomes children.

Route 2 **6½ miles**

Tunnel End and Standedge

Outline Tunnel End Visitor Centre—Redbrook Reservoir—Standedge—Rapes Highway—Eastergate Bridge—Hey Green—Tunnel End.

Summary This walk starting in the upper Colne Valley is perhaps best left for the more experienced family group, since for the most part it crosses exposed moorland and wild country at the south-western-most outpost of the county. The compensations are many though, with extensive panoramas along a route which follows parts of the Pennine Way and ancient packhorse trails, even making a brief inroad into the Peak District National Park.

Attractions For the lover of wild, open spaces this walk is a must. The South Pennines offer a rugged landscape to rival better known districts and here the gritstone scarp of Standedge provides views across Diggle into the Greater Manchester district and South Yorkshire.

Marsden is a typical Pennine hill town with contour-hugging stone cottages and classic mill architecture. Further up the Colne Valley the hamet of Tunnel End achieved fame as the point where the Huddersfield narrow canal and the Leeds to Manchester railway line dive beneath the Pennines, to emerge 3¼ miles later at Diggle. It is the longest canal tunnel in Britain and took 18 years to complete, opening in 1811 and closing in 1944. Because it lacks a tow path the bargees had to lie on their back on the barges and punt them along the ceiling, a process known as 'legging'.

Marsden Moor is now owned by the National Trust and is criss-crossed by many ancient byways. Comprising some 5685 acres of natural moorland, it provides habitat to many ground nesting birds, including Dunlin, Golden Plover, Snipe and Meadow Pipit.

After tracing the Pennine Way almost 2 miles along Standedge to the north-western extremity of this walk the packhorse trail of Rapes Highway is followed back into the upper Colne Valley, entering Hey Green via Willykay Clough where the quaint Eastergate packhorse bridge spans the beck. This is now listed as an ancient monument.

At Tunnel End there are displays relating the story of the Standedge tunnels, while on the nearby dam may be seen ducks and other water birds.

Refreshments The Junction Inn at Tunnel End. There is also a small shop within the Visitor Centre. Picnic areas are provided nearby.

Route 2

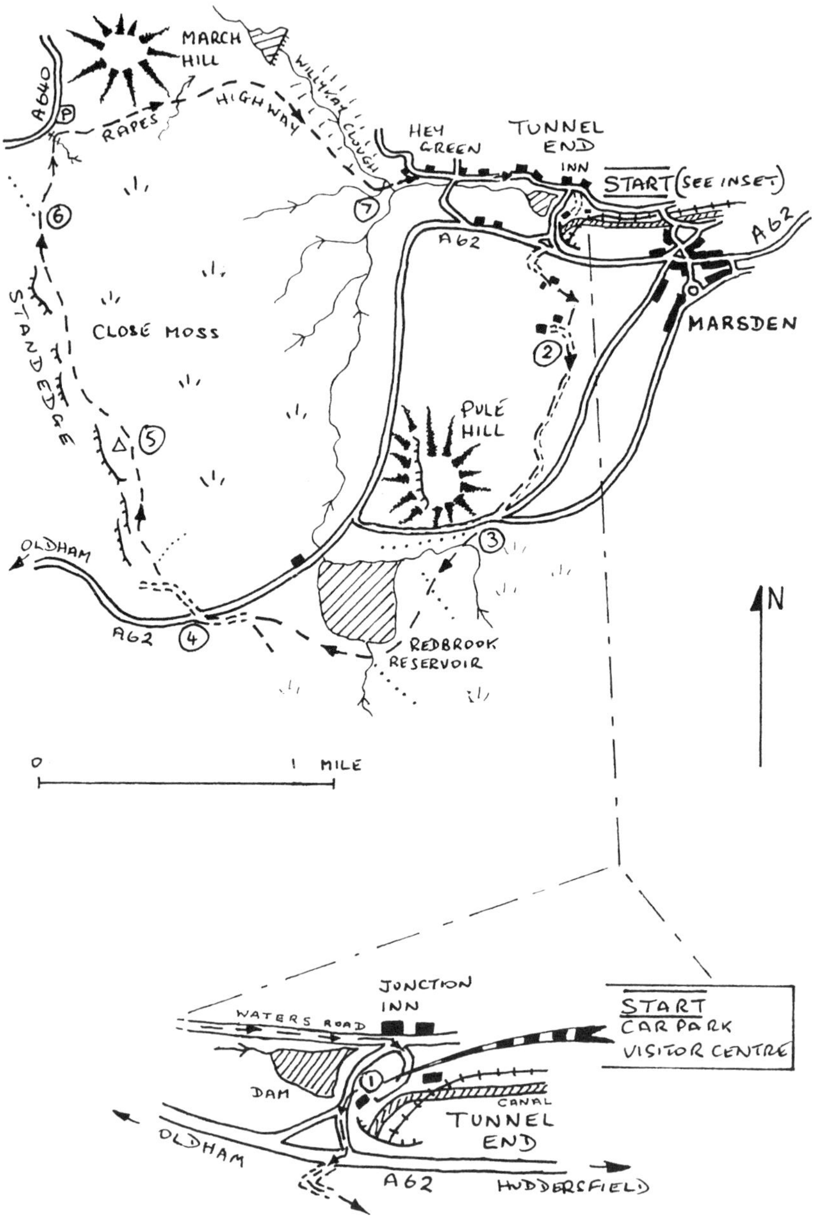
MARCH HILL
A640
P
RAPES HIGHWAY
WILLYKAY CLOUGH
HEY GREEN
TUNNEL END
INN
START (SEE INSET)
A62
A62
MARSDEN
CLOSE MOSS
STANDEDGE
PULE HILL
OLDHAM
A62
REDBROOK RESERVOIR
N
0
1 MILE
JUNCTION INN
WATERS ROAD
START
CAR PARK
VISITOR CENTRE
DAM
CANAL
TUNNEL END
OLDHAM
A62
HUDDERSFIELD

Route 2

Tunnel End and Standedge — 6½ miles

START: *Tunnel End, This is just off the A62 Huddersfield to Oldham trans-Pennine road and is reached by way of a short unclassified lane 10 miles out of Huddersfield. Park adjacent to the Visitor Centre (G.R. SE040119). O.S. Landranger sheet 110 (Sheffield and Huddersfield).*

ROUTE

1. *Take the path up the steps from the car park leading behind the visitor centre to reach and cross a stile. Turn left then left at the fork in the lane to reach the A62. Turn right, cross the road and walk left up the first stony track to a farm after ¼ mile. Go through a small gate in the wall on your left, then bear right between the two houses. Continue forward following a vague field path, then at a point 25 yards down from the right corner cross a wall (no stile), stride over the gulley and climb a bank to stile. Go over this, fording a small stream to cross a second stile. Walk beside a wall through a gate then a gap in a fence, before turning right uphill.*
2. *Go through a gate at the farm to follow a track to a tarmac road after ¾ mile. Turn right to a junction a few yards ahead.*
3. *Cross the road and descend a ditch. Climb the banking and turn right along an obvious moorland path. Ignore a track descending from the left ¾ mile ahead, and continue around the south side of Redbrook Reservoir. Eventually the path meets the A62 where this intersects the Pennine Way.*
4. *Cross the road and follow the stony track, the route of both the Pennine and Oldham Ways. After 250 yards leave the track and climb a rocky bank on your right to a path heading for some ruined walls. At the first of these ignore a path going right, instead veering left at a fingerpost to cross a stile. A second stile is crossed after 60 yards and the path followed to the triangulation pillar on Standedge.*
5. *Continue for another mile to where the way ahead divides where a small stream flows from a peat bank on your right.*
6. *Turn right along a gravel path* ***(note the post with yellow arrow)*** *eventually descending to a footbridge by the A640. Cross the bridge and turn right back up the hill to follow a packhorse trail* ***(Rapes Highway).*** *This soon descends towards Hey Green.*
7. *At the bottom of Willykay Clough cross the packhorse bridge and turn right, following the beckside to a gate. Go through the gate and turn right down Waters Road to return to Tunnel End.*

ACCESS BY BUS/TRAIN

Train or Yorkshire Rider bus services 350, 351, 352 and 365 from Huddersfield to Marsden, then a 10 minute stroll along the towpath to Tunnel End.

PACKHORSE BRIDGE, BECKFOOT (Route 7)

Route 3 **5½ miles**

(shorter variation 4¼ miles)

Stoodley Pike and Rochdale Canal

Outline Rochdale Canal—Calderdale Way—Mankinholes—Pannier Trail—Pennine Way—Stoodley Pike—Edge End Moor—Rochdale Canal.

Summary This excellent route takes in several periods of transport history, from canal scenery and paved pannier ways to the more recent long distance pathways devised primarily for walkers. The ground is varied and in places exposed but always good underfoot, taking in gritstone moors, woods and towpaths. The Stoodley Pike monument offers fine views of the district and beyond.

Attractions After a short stretch along the Rochdale Canal the Calderdale Way climbs towards the open fells. As height is gained fine views unfold on all points of the compass. To the north Bridestones Moor is seen as a wild backdrop to Todmorden with the Calder Valley drawing the eye east towards Heptonstall and Hebden Bridge.

On the approach to Mankinholes, Stoodley Pike comes into view on the ridgeline over to your left. The sleepy hamlet was once a moorland bastion of early Quakerism and isolated enough to be passed by when the Industrial Revolution came to Calderdale. Industry here was confined to the spinning wheel and handloom, the highlight of Pennine life being the occasional visit from the travelling broggers with their colourful pack ponies.

Leaving Mankinholes and heading south an ambitious pannier way wends its way steeply up the flank of Langfield Common. It is paved throughout to improve the traction for pack ponies. The old trail is left to continue its journey to Cragg Vale, haunt of a notorious 18th century counterfeiting gang, while a windswept scarp edge leads to Stoodley Pike. The path winds its way between grit slabs reminiscent of the fallen and blackened tombstones of ancient warriors.

Stoodley Pike was built to celebrate the surrender of Paris after the battle of Waterloo. A magnificent 360 degree panorama may be enjoyed by climbing the dark staircase within the monument to gain a viewing balcony above. You may care to carry a torch for this; however it is perfectly safe to allow the children to explore in total darkness. The view (on a clear day that is) includes Emley Moor, Nab Hill, Quensbury, Boulsworth Hill and Blackstone Edge.

After savouring the scenery a quick descent arrives at a parting of the ways at a track known as London Road. Decision time, a short route back to the start, or a longer way avoiding tarmac lanes and offering a more

continued on page 20

Route 3

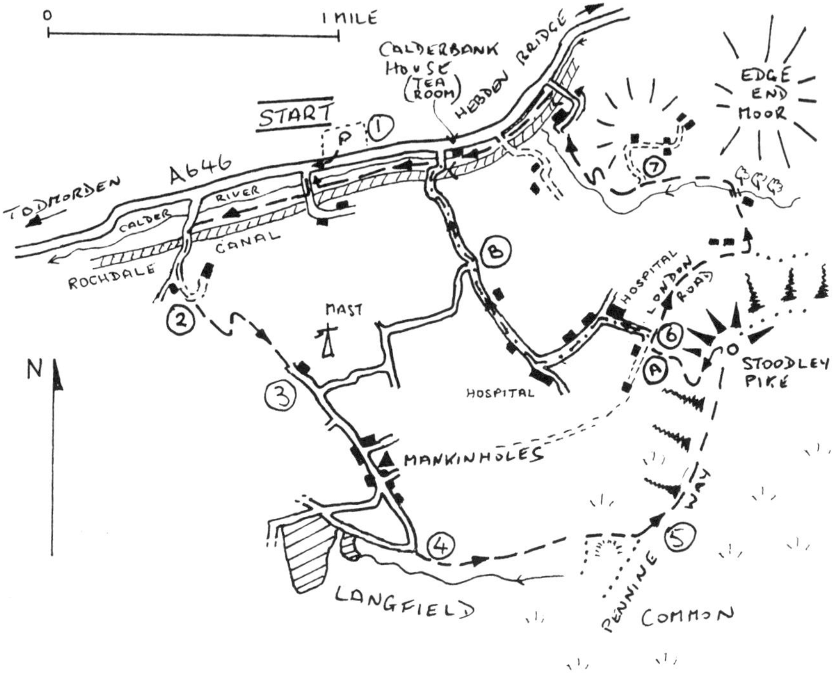

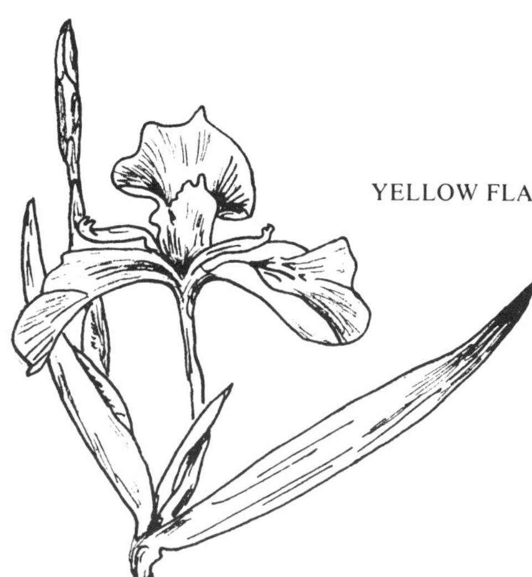

YELLOW FLAG yellow June–Aug

Route 3

Stoodley Pike and Rochdale Canal — 5½ miles

(shorter variation 4¼ miles)

START: *Park at the picnic area beside the Castle Street railway Viaduct just off the A646 Hebden Bridge to Todmorden road 1½ miles east of the latter. O.S. Landranger map sheet 103 (Blackburn and Burnley). G.R. 956247.*

ROUTE:

1. *Turn right out of the car park and along the road towards Todmorden. After 100 yards turn left up Haugh Road, then right on to the canal towpath and follow this to the next bridge. Take the steps up to the right and turn left across the bridge, following the lane to a fork.*
2. *Turn left up a dirt track* ***(Calderdale Way)*** *to a sharp bend left. Continue straight on along a wall side to a stile on your left after 6 yards. Cross this and follow an ascending path to your right. Pass through a gap in the wall and trace the path winding its way uphill to a stile. Cross the stile to follow the obvious field path, with a radio mast seen ahead, and reach a broken wall. Cross the stile and head for the far left corner of the next field. Go through the stile here* ***(signposted Mankinholes)*** *and, with a wall on your left, make for a farm.*
3. *Keeping the farm on your left walk down the stony track to a metalled road. Continue forward through Mankinoles and, where the road turns right, walk forward on dirt road to reach a stile.*
4. *Cross the stile and turn left along a paved packhorse trail climbing to the scarp edge. Near the top the trail turns sharp right. Leave the trail here and continue ahead along a path that skirts some spoil heaps and joins the Pennine Way at the scarp edge.*
5. *Follow this left with level going as far as the monument. Outside the entrance to the monument take a steep path which descends to a fence by a farm.*
6. *Ignore the stile here to turn right along a bridleway* ***(London Road).*** *Follow this for ½ mile to a fork. Turn left towards a farm, then bear right along the side of the wall. Turn left through a gate after 130 yards and, with a ruined farmhouse on your right, head for a bridge over a wooded gill* ***(picnic spot).*** *Cross this and, where the track levels out, turn left down a footpath which passes through a line of trees and a broken wall to reach a gate at a fence.*
7. *Go through the gate and walk along a dirt road going downhill through a wooded clough* ***(picnic spots)*** *to a gate by some terraced houses. Go*

through the gate and follow the metalled lane to the canal at Homecot Locks. Turn left and follow the towpath for ¾ mile to Mill Lock. Walk up onto the bridge, turn right and at the main road turn right to return to car park.

Shorter Variation

A. As for 1 to 6 above, then cross the stile and walk down to a farm track. Turn right then left and follow the track to a 'T' junction by the Fielden Hospital. Turn left along the metalled lane, then right at the next junction, following the road to a fork.

B. Continue straight forward downhill to the canal at Shawplain Lock. Turn left along the towpath to Mill Lock in a little less than ½ mile. Walk up onto the bridge, turn right and at the main road turn right to return to the car park.

ACCESS BY BUS/TRAIN

Metro operate buses half hourly between Todmorden and Hebden Bridge. Service Nos. 590 and 592.

---

picturesque and varied return journey amid woodlands and further picturesque reaches of the canal. Through Calderdale this is mostly disused and slowly being reclaimed by nature. It is overgrown in places with yellow flag and a haven for mallard, moorhen, coot and other creatures.

Refreshments Calderbank House, by Shawplains Locks, offers lunches, tea garden and play area. The longer option for return passes one or two places ideal for picnic halts.

Route 4 **6½ miles**

Crimsworth Dean and Hardcastle Crags

Outline Gibson Mill—Shackleton Wood—New Bridge—Crimsworth Dean—Lumb Falls—Abel Cross—Hardcastle Crags—Gibson Mill

Summary This is a superb family outing taking in some of the finest walking in West Yorkshire, much of it on good paths maintained by the National Trust. Both Crimsworth Dean and Hardcastle Crags are areas that full justify their popularity, both for the scenic beauty and the richness of its wildlife. The route mostly follows bridleways or valley bottom trails through mixed woodlands, with one section over open country by the Kid Stones. Best reserved for a hot summer day.

Attractions The great surprise for many first time visitors to West Yorkshire is the fact that there is so much fine and varied scenery. This route combines some of the best, beginning with a descending trail into Hebden Hey at the disused Gibson Mill.

This is named after Abraham Gibson who owned a cotton spinning business at nearby Greenwood. The mill was once powered by a 5 horse-power water wheel, until manufacturing ceased in the late 19th century. Hebden Water is crossed at a bridge by the mill, fortunately no longer subject to the toll charge once demanded of bygone travellers. As an alternative to the bridge the children may care to test their skill on the hippings (stepping stones) a few yards downstream.

Much of this valley and neighbouring Crimsworth Dean was planted as an attraction for Lord Saville's shooting estate. Hardcastle Crags is the subject of a Nature Trail (leaflets from the Tourist Information Office in Hebden Bridge). There are deer, fox, squirrel and abundant birdlife.

Tree creepers and especially dippers are easily spotted, but see if you can espy the great spotted and green woodpecker or a rare species of carnivorous wood ant which makes its nests from pine needles.

From Gibson Mill a well worn beckside path is traced down valley through light woodland dominated by Scots Pine. In spring the undergrowth is dotted with the bright 'eyes' of anemones and sorrel or suffused with the dreamy blue haze of wild hyacinth. After ½ mile a second set of stepping stones leads to the far bank of the stream and a track leading to New Bridge, a quiet little corner in a hamlet quaintly known as Midgehole.

At this point there is an abrupt change of direction as the Calderdale Way long distance path is briefly followed. This departs for Pecket Well leaving field paths to continue almost two miles north into Crimsworth

continued on page 24

Route 4

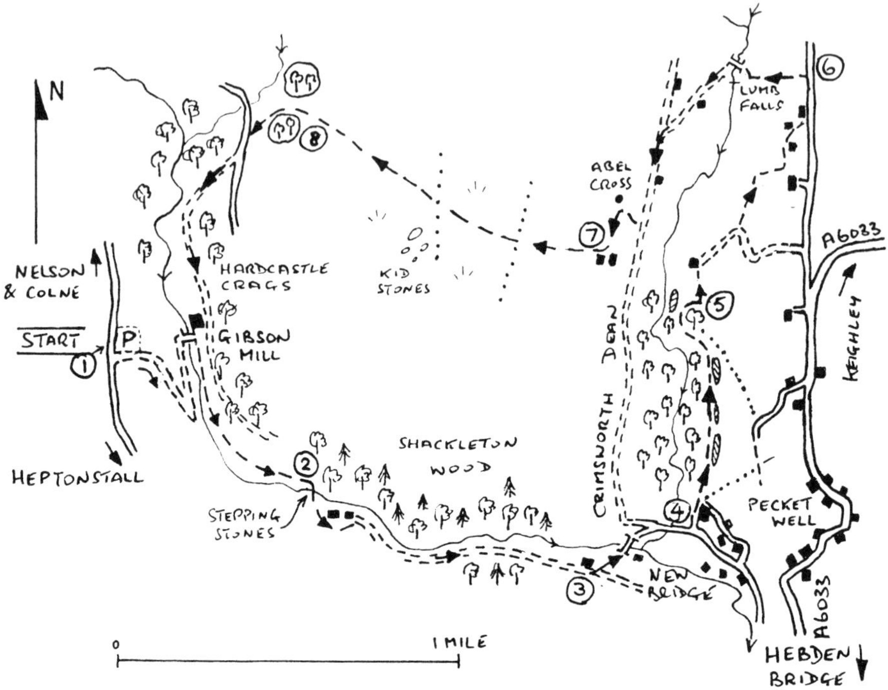

DIPPER 18cm brown/white/chestnut

Route 4

Crimsworth Dean and Hardcastle Crags 6½ miles

START: *The National Trust car park and picnic site provided at G.R. SD969298 on the Hebden Bridge to Colne road 1½ miles south of Widdop gate. O.S. Landranger Series sheet 103 (Blackburn and Burnley).*

ROUTE

1. *From the car park follow a path leading behind the information plaque bearing right then left down a stony track. This zig-zags down the valley side to a bridge by Gibson Mill. Cross the bridge and turn right. Ignore a track bearing half left to follow a trail keeping close to the stream.*
2. *After ½ mile cross to the far bank by way of some stepping stones and follow an ascending path to your left. Follow this behind the scout hostel and descend the concrete steps to reach the dirt access road. Walk along this to a point 200 yards after Howden Hall.*
3. *Descend a path to your left. At the bottom turn left across the river bridge to reach a road junction. Turn right and look for a path signposted Calderdale Way.*
4. *Turn left along this path and where the track bends to the right follow a field path* ***(signposted Haworth Old Road)*** *straight ahead. This soon levels out to a gate. Go through this and head uphill to the corner of a small dam on your right. Climb the wall corner to follow the path alongside a series of disused dams and water cuts. At the iron railing walk to your right and follow a path up through trees to a wall. Follow this uphill to a gate.*
5. *Turn left through the gate following a field path to a farm. Go through a gate here and walk up the track as far as an acute bend. Take the path on the left to a stile in a wall. Cross this and, with a wall on your left, continue for 50 yards. Turn right uphill towards a farm and, when level with the buildings, turn left into wall corner and cross a stile. Walk forward with the next farm on your right and cross a second stile. Bearing right of the next building enter a lane by the next farmhouse, proceeding up this to the road. Turn left and follow this for 100 yards to a bridleway on the left.*
6. *Follow the bridleway and cross a packhorse bridge. Ascend the path* ***(signposted Hardcastle Crags)*** *passing a ruined barn and turn left along a track. After about ½ mile turn right along a farm access track.*
7. *Just before a farm turn uphill to your right* ***(path not obvious)*** *over the skyline to reach a wall. Go through a gate, continuing forward on a*

track, passing a water trough, and downhill to fence. Cross the stile here and head for the gap between two small woods to find a second stile.

8. *Cross this and continue in the same direction to enter the lane to New Laith Moor. Turn left then right at the first fork, following the track downhill to Gibson Mill. Turn right across bridge and ascend track back to the start in the car park.*

Dean. At Lumb Falls a packhorse bridge leads to a steep but short path joining the green lane of Haworth Old Road.

The ancient Abel Cross marks where the route departs for open country past the Kid Stones and returns to Gibson Mill via Hardcastle Crags. Unfortunately the altitude lost at the start of the walk now has to be regained to return to the car park.

Refreshments There are no pubs or cafes on route, so a packed lunch is recommended. Being approximately half way, Lumb Falls is an ideal place for a picnic stop.

TOP WITHENS

Route 5 **7 miles**

On the Brontë Trail

Outline Haworth—Penistone Hill—Brontë Falls and Bridge—Withens—Stanbury—Lumb Foot—Haworth.

Summary A fine walk that will inspire the literary minded. Haworth of course is steeped in history, the perfect springboard for exploring the neighbouring moors. The walk has the feel of a real expedition about it, while Brontë Bridge and the ruined farmhouse of Withens provide the younger members of the group with the opportunity to clamber and explore.

Attractions Haworth is a fine example of Yorkshire hill village, focused on its cobbled main street rising like a steep canyon amid a medley of tiny shops and cafes. It clings fortress like to the edge of those wind-swept moors that inspired its famous author sisters.

The village grew from the thriving cottage industry of the 18th century, when at its height, around 1840, there was an incredible 1200 weaving looms operating in Haworth. One can see the school where Charlotte Brontë taught, or browse around the Parsonage which retains much of the atmosphere, and furnishings from the time when it was the Brontë home.

Children will find the stocks by the church an amusement and the numerous ginnels and alleyways provide opportunities to explore before venturing on to the moors. Apart from its literary associations Haworth is of course home to the Keighley Worth Valley Steam Railway. Steam loco hauled passenger trains operate regularly between Keighley and Oxenhope stopping of course at Haworth.

Though there is much to dwell upon in Haworth and the steamers are an enduring attraction, the bustle of a high season day will drive any discerning rambler to the open spaces. The abode of the curlew calls out with that same spirit that gave the English speaking world those much loved novels and characters.

From the outskirts of the village a pathway leads quickly to the summit of Penistone Hill, giving open vistas across Lower Laithe Reservoir to Stanbury and beyond. Good going leads from here to Sladen Beck spanned by Brontë Bridge, a favourite haunt of both Emily and Charlotte and a good place to call a lunch halt. Nearby is Brontë Falls, though this is rather disappointing except after heavy rain.

The route gradually gains altitude among moors which in September are aglow with flowering ling. The solitary ruin of Withens appears on the skyline, said by some historians to be the inspiration for Wuthering Heights.

continued on page 28

Route 5

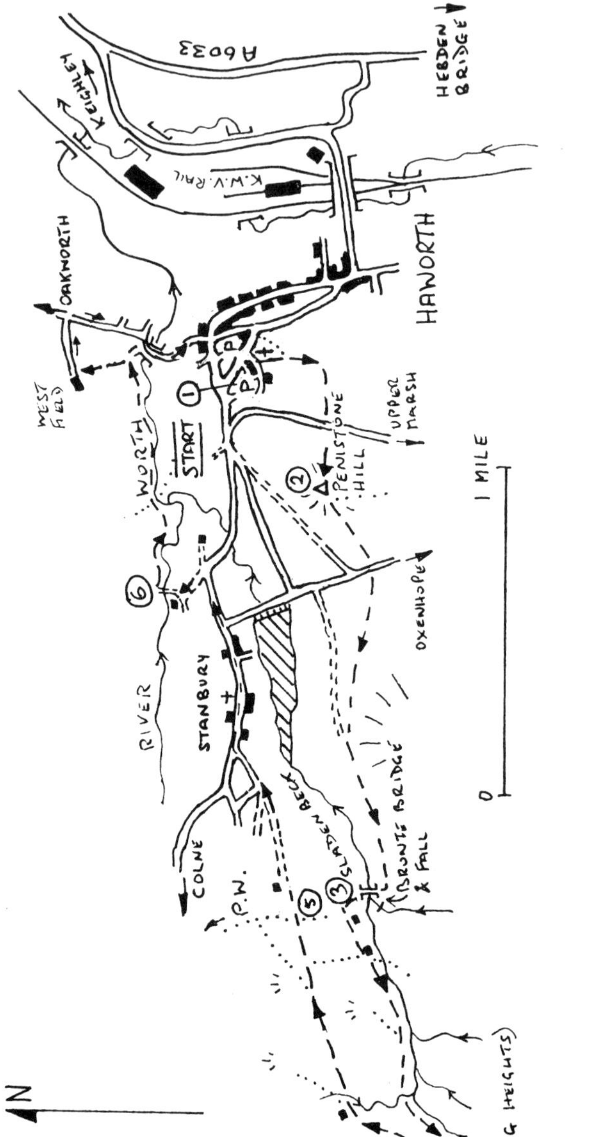

A6033
KEIGHLEY
HEBDEN BRIDGE
K.W.V. RAIL
OAKWORTH
HAWORTH
WEST FIELD
WORTH
START
P
1
UPPER MARSH
2
PENISTONE HILL
1 MILE
0
OXENHOPE
6
STANBURY
RIVER
SLADEN BECK
BRONTE BRIDGE & FALL
3
5
COLNE
P.W.
N
4
TOP WITHENS (WUTHERING HEIGHTS)
P.W.

Route 5

On the Brontë Trail 7 miles

START: *Haworth is situated just off the A6033 Keighley to Hebden Bridge road. Ample parking is available off West Lane at the north end of town. G.R. SE029374. O.S. Landranger sheets 104 (Leeds and Bradford) and 103 (Blackburn and Burnley).*

ROUTE

1. *Turn right out of the car park down West Lane and right up the lane towards the Brontë Parsonage. Take the first left after the church along a path* ***(signposted the moors and Penistone Hill).*** *Cross the road to Upper Marsh and follow a path to the summit of Penistone Hill.*
2. *From the triangulation pillar a well marked route continues west, across the Stanbury to Oxenhope moor road and contours around Enshaw Knoll to join a track from your right. This eventually descends to Sladen Beck at Brontë Bridge, three miles into the walk.*
3. *Cross the bridge and, climbing steeply up the valley side, bear left along a path passing a ruined farm. Cross the next two walls* ***(stiles provided)*** *and at the second ruined building ignore a path down to the left and continue forward. After a further ¼ mile the path descends and crosses a stream, then climbs to join the Pennine Way at Withens.*
4. *Turn right along the well trod path and, by a second building about ¼ mile ahead, fork right for ¾ mile to where the P.W. turns left.*
5. *Continue ahead, soon entering a lane through Cold Knoll to a road junction. Turn right and ½ mile beyond Stanbury turn left down a steep stony track to Lumb Foot. Bear right at the bottom and cross the bridge.*
6. *Turn right and follow the River Worth for one mile. Just before the road bridge turn left and climb towards West Field. Join a track here and turn right into Mytholmes Lane, tracing this uphill to a junction in Haworth. Turn right along North Street then left along West Lane to the start.*

ACCESS BY BUS/TRAIN

There are regular bus services from Keighley to Oxenhope calling at Haworth. The K.W.V.Railway operates between Keighley and Haworth.

From this point it is but a brief journey as the broomstick flies, across the Forest of Trawden to Pendle Hill, deep in the heart of witch country.

From Withens the Pennine Way leads off in the direction of Stanbury, once the village home of Timmy Feather, last of the district's handloom weavers. Inside the church is the Reverend Patrick Brontë's pulpit taken from the old Haworth church prior to its demolition.

East of Stanbury a path leading via Lumb Foot follows the River Worth downstream on the return leg to Haworth.

Refreshments The White Lion in Haworth has a children's room. There are several cafes too.

GOIT STOCK FALLS

Route 6 **3½ miles**

Harden and Goit Stock Waterfall

Outline Leech Lane—Harden Beck—Goit Stock Waterfall—Harden Beck—Harden Bridge—Leech Lane.

Summary An excellent half day outing offering easy going with no steep gradients, mostly through broad leaf woodlands and along farm tracks and field paths. Plenty of beckside locations for play, paddling and stick dipping. Almost anywhere along Harden Beck is ideal for a picnic stop and provides a chance to look out for dippers and other birds.

Attractions This is a route dominated by woodlands through which Harden Beck is traced along a serpentine course on its way to join the Aire. Spring or autumn are the best times of year for this route. The only blot on the landscape as the walker descends Leech Lane is the sight of electricity pylons marching across the valley.

After skirting the edges of a caravan park, field paths pass by a solitary chimney, then cross a small tributary beck at a clapper bridge, an excellent spot to dally for lunch, before striking off through the middle of a forest clearing.

The oak and silver birch woods that follow are carpeted with brambles and bracken. Soon the sound of Harden Beck over to your left lures the walker from his route ahead. In fact the head of Goit Stock waterfall can be reached at this point. However, it is far better to resist the temptation to deviate and continue along the path.

When returning along the opposite bank, the cataract may be seen to advantage and in complete safety. It is an impressive sight, especially following heavy rain, when the rocky amphitheatre acts like a megaphone amplifying the noise of the 20ft cascade.

Continuing downstream the sound of falling water is soon left behind. Holly and birch provide sparse cover in a landscape dotted with the occasional gritstone boulder. See how many species of bird can be spotted along this stretch of the route.

The walk continues in similar vein before emerging at Harden Bridge, from where farm tracks and field paths return to the start by way of Leech Lane.

Refreshments The Malt Shovel pub at Harden Bridge. Children allowed in snug. Outside play area.

Route 6

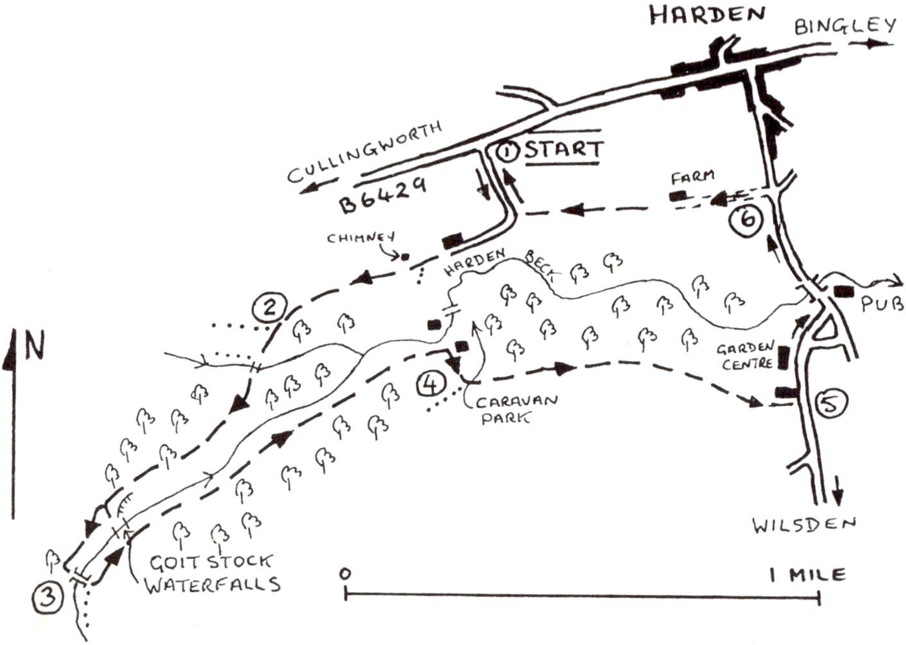

THE PANCAKE STONE (Route 8)

18th Nov '94. Boys thought it was too long
Nice day ≃ 2½ - 3hrs.

Route 6

Harden and Goit Stock Waterfall — 3½ miles

START: *A lay-by on the B6429 Bingley to Cullingworth road at Leech Lane a half mile west of Harden. (G.R. SE079379) O.S. Landranger sheet 104 (Leeds and Bradford).*

ROUTE

1. *Turn left down Leech Lane, following it around the bend to a gate. Go through the gate and, with cottages on your right, walk ahead through a second gate to where the path divides after 40 yards. Bear right to a third gate and stile. Cross this and take the path passing a chimney to reach a wall corner. With the wall on your left, walk forward to a gate and stile where a path takes off to the right.* Went wrong here.
2. *Walk down the wall side to a small brook. Cross a clapper bridge and walk to the right, up the bank, to a wall corner. Climb a few steps here and head off across a forest clearing to the far right corner. Cross a stile and continue for ¼ mile to a fence at the edge of the woods. Cross a stile here and bear left to cross a second stile, then turn right to a footbridge.*
3. *Cross the bridge and turn immediately left along the path following the opposite bank and soon descending to where Goit Stock Waterfall cascades 20 feet into a rocky cove. For the next ½ mile the route takes a beckside course through light woodland.*
4. *At a cottage, take the path climbing to the right, then left at the bottom of the garden to reach a wall after 200 yards. Turn left beside this and walk beneath an electricity pylon, continuing for ½ mile to a stile. Cross this. With a fence on your left, proceed through a gate hole, then along a wall side to a gap stile at the main road.*
5. *Turn left and, just past the garden centre, walk forward down Mill Hill Top* **(signposted access only).** *At the bottom of the hill turn left over Harden Bridge by the Malt Shovel and walk up the hill for 260 yards to a track on the left.*
6. *Turn left down the track* **(signposted),** *and keeping a farm on your right, walk forward to a gate hole. Go through this and follow the wall side until this ends. From here make a beeline for a power line pole, ford a small brook and continue forward uphill through hawthorn bushes to the acute bend in Leech Lane. Turn right and return to the start.*

ACCESS BY BUS

Keighley and District bus service No. 727 and 728 from Bingley to Cullingworth passes Leech Lane.

MARKET HALL, BINGLEY

Route 7 **5 miles**
(shorter variation 4¼ miles)

Bingley and the Druid's Altar

Outline Bingley Market Hall—Mill Gate—Ireland Bridge—Raven Royd—Marley—Druid's Altar—-Beckfoot—Bingley Market Hall.

Summary This is a fine walk for all the family with much to interest Mum and Dad as well as the children. Starting in the town of Bingley, this varied circular route enjoys both high and low level scenery of Airedale taking in a forgotten domesday hamlet. Good paths provide easy walking throughout, except for one steep section to the Druid's Altar. At the half-way point there are expansive views along the length of Airedale, followed by a mixture of ancient highways and riverside paths returning via Beckfoot packhorse bridge to the start.

Attractions Bingley is an ancient township, receiving its first Market Charter in the year 1212. Adjacent to the car park where this walk begins may be seen the old Market Hall, Butter Cross and village stocks, relocated here following restoration.

At the outset the route follows the High Street as far as the oldest part of town, known as Bailey Hills. The nearby church dates mostly from the reign of Henry VIII and is certainly worth a visit. Inside may be seen stained glass by William Morris, the remains of a Saxon or Danish cross, a fine rood screen and the famous Rune Stone, a font-like basin bearing strange carvings.

Because of its picturesque surroundings Bingley was once referred to as the 'Throstle-nest of old England'. Notwithstanding the fact that the railway, the Leeds to Liverpool canal and the A650 divide the town, one may still discover some pleasant rural backwaters just a stone's throw from its busy centre.

One of the highlights of this walk is the Druid's Altar, a gritstone outcrop located to the west of and easily reached from town. Leaving the church, Ireland Bridge takes the walker across the river Aire past the Brown Cow pub where the Bingley Petty Sessions were once held. From here a stony track through Altar Wood leads to Marley, settlement mentioned in the 1066 Domesday Survey.

A stiff climb up the valley side compensates with views extending across to Rombald's Moor and up the dale as far as Malham Moor. Level going soon reaches the altar stone. It's an evocative spot, perhaps best visited on a day when storm clouds hang overhead like harbingers of certain doom. On

continued on page 36

Route 7

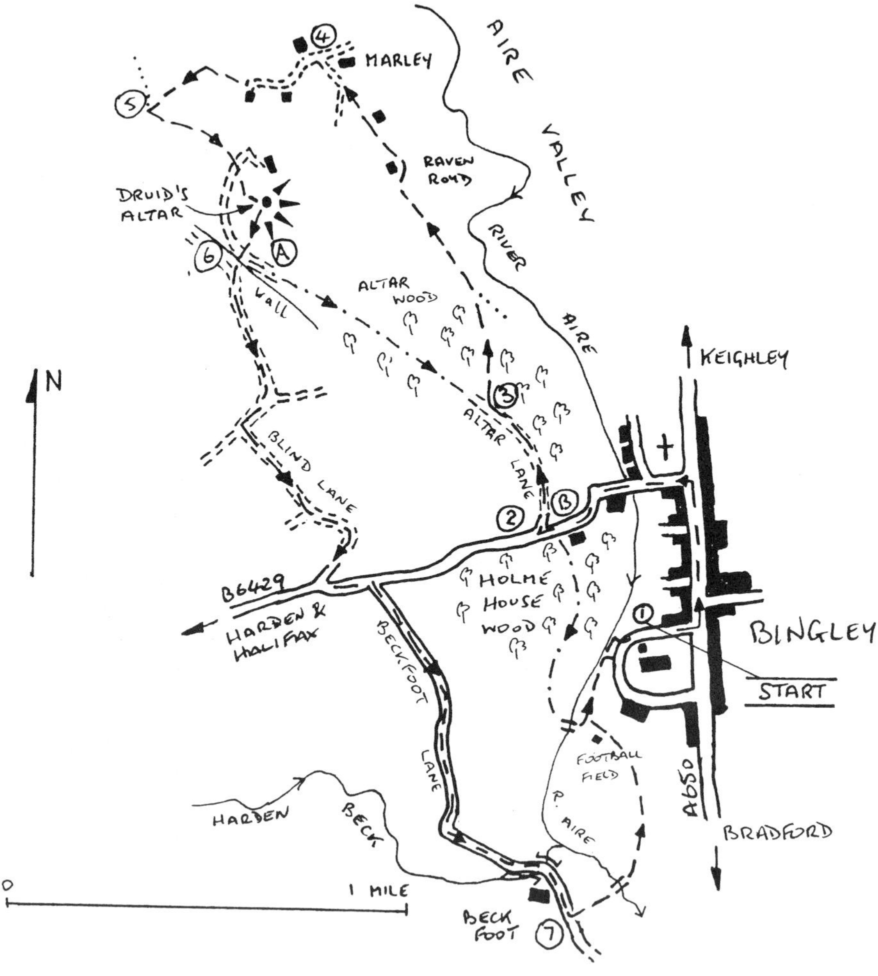

AIRE VALLEY
MARLEY
RAVEN ROYD
DRUID'S ALTAR
WALL
ALTAR WOOD
RIVER AIRE
KEIGHLEY
N
ALTAR LANE
BLIND LANE
B6429
HARDEN & HALIFAX
HOLME HOUSE WOOD
BECKFOOT LANE
BINGLEY
START
FOOTBALL FIELD
R. AIRE
A650
HARDEN BECK
BRADFORD
0
1 MILE
BECK FOOT

Route 7
Bingley and the Druid's Altar **5 miles**

(shorter variation 4¼ miles)

START: *At Bingley located on the A65 midway between Keighley and Shipley. Parking is available adjacent to the old market hall and cross near the Bingley Little Theatre. G.R. SE106390, O.S. Landranger sheet 104 (Leeds and Bradford).*

ROUTE

1. *From the car park walk along Queens Street and left down the High Street to the traffic lights just before Mill Gate. Turn left across the river and follow the road uphill to Altar Lane.*
2. *Turn right and follow the stony track through woods for ¼ mile to a junction with a path.*
3. *Bear right and descend to meet another track at river level. Bear left and continue to Raven Royd. With the building on your left follow a cobbled lane to a walled lane. Walk along this past a ruined farm to reach a gate after 130 yards. Go through this and follow a track to another gate after which the way forks. Take the left branch along wall side to reach yet another gate. Beyond this, bear right through a kissing gate where Marley comes into view. Follow the track right then left into a lane ending at a gate and stile.*
4. *Go through the stile and turn left. Cross a ford and follow a winding track uphill. At the next farm keep right through a gate and continue to another farm. Here the way bears left with steep climbing to a wall. Go through a stile and continue forward, still climbing. When the going levels out another path is met.*
5. *Turn left, ignoring a stile in the wall on your right after 150 yards. After a further ½ mile cross a step stile and shortly afterwards meet a stony track from left. Cross this and follow a path to the Druids Altar, beyond which the path returns to the track at a stile in a high wall.*
6. *Cross the stile and turn left, following a track downhill to Blind Lane. Turn left here and at the bottom turn left down the B6429. Turn right along Beckfoot Lane, following this to a ford and bridge about ½ mile ahead.*
7. *Cross the bridge and walk between the buildings to pick up a footpath left to a river bridge. Cross this and follow the path along the right hand side of a football field towards a shelter. Just beyond this turn right along the riverbank, and just beyond a pipeline across the river, turn right and climb the steps back to car park.*

SHORTER ALTERNATIVE

As for 1 to 6 above then:

A. Instead of crossing the stile bear left down Altar Lane to the B6429.

B. Cross the road and take the footpath down alongside a fence, following this through Holme House Wood to cross a footbridge over the river. Turn left along the river bank to reach the steps returning to the car park.

ACCESS BY BUS/TRAIN

There are regular train services linking all Airedale towns with Bingley. Bus services Nos. 662–668 from Bradford and 760 from Leeds.

---

such occasions it takes little stretch of a child's fertile imagination to visualise the Celtic High Priests bent on some Fell deed.

The track running along the scarp edge was originally a pre-Turnpike road, the main route in fact between Scotland, the north and the wool towns of the West Riding. Lord Clifford probably passed this way in 1526 while on route between Skipton Castle and London.

The descending track is traced back to Beckfoot, where a ford and packhorse bridge lead to a route across the Aire and a quick return to the start.

Refreshments The Fleece (beer garden), the Brown Cow (outside tables) and Old Queens Head (childrens' room) all in Bingley.

Mike, Matt & me – Wed 25/10/95. Parts of walk.

Route 8 **4¼ miles**

Ilkley Moor and Twelve Apostles

Outline Cow and Calf Rocks—Pancake Stone—Gill Head—Twelve Apostles—Gill Head—White Wells—Cow and Calf Rocks

Summary This is a fine introduction to moorland walking before perhaps going on to attempt route number two in this guide. Good walking prevails and should present no difficulties, though if misty the many pathways could confuse. There are plenty of unusual rock formations and good scrambling for any budding rock climbers.

Attractions Ilkley Moor is just one small part of the more expansive Rombald's Moor, named after a giant said by tradition to have roamed the area. The moor is steeped in history, where 7,000 years of habitation by man is etched indelibly into the landscape.

The walk begins at a roadside car park at Cow and Calf Rocks, then climbs to the scarp edge. There are many unusual rock formations on route, such as the Pancake Stone, Badger Stone, the famous Cow and Calf Rocks. Perhaps more intriguing are the enigmatic cup and ring marked rocks. These strange rock carvings are to be found all over the moor, with over 200 sites identified.

Though these are known to date from the Bronze Age their purpose remains one of life's intractable mysteries. One of the greatest concentrations of these stones is to be found along Green Crag Slack, between the Pancake Stone and Backstone Beck. See how many you can discover, though it isn't easy because of the covering of heather.

Easy walking on obvious paths leads from the Pancake Stone to an even more intriguing group of stones. The Twelve Apostles is a stone circle located on the eastern extremity of the main ridge. This too is of Bronze Age origins and was perhaps used as a ceremonial enclosure.

Ilkley rose to fame as a centre for salubrity from the late 18th through to mid-19th centuries. The hydropathic method of treating illnesses, popular in Victorian times, resulted in the town becoming the health spa of the north. People came from far and wide to 'take the waters'.

After marvelling at the stone circle the moorland path, provided in places with boardwalk to combat erosion, descends to a cairn above Ilkley Crag. The views are magnificent, up and down the dale and across to Denton Moor. Higher up the fell the range extends beyond the radar dishes at Menwith Hill to the White Horse of Kilburn at the edge of the Hambleton Hills.

continued on page 40

Route 8

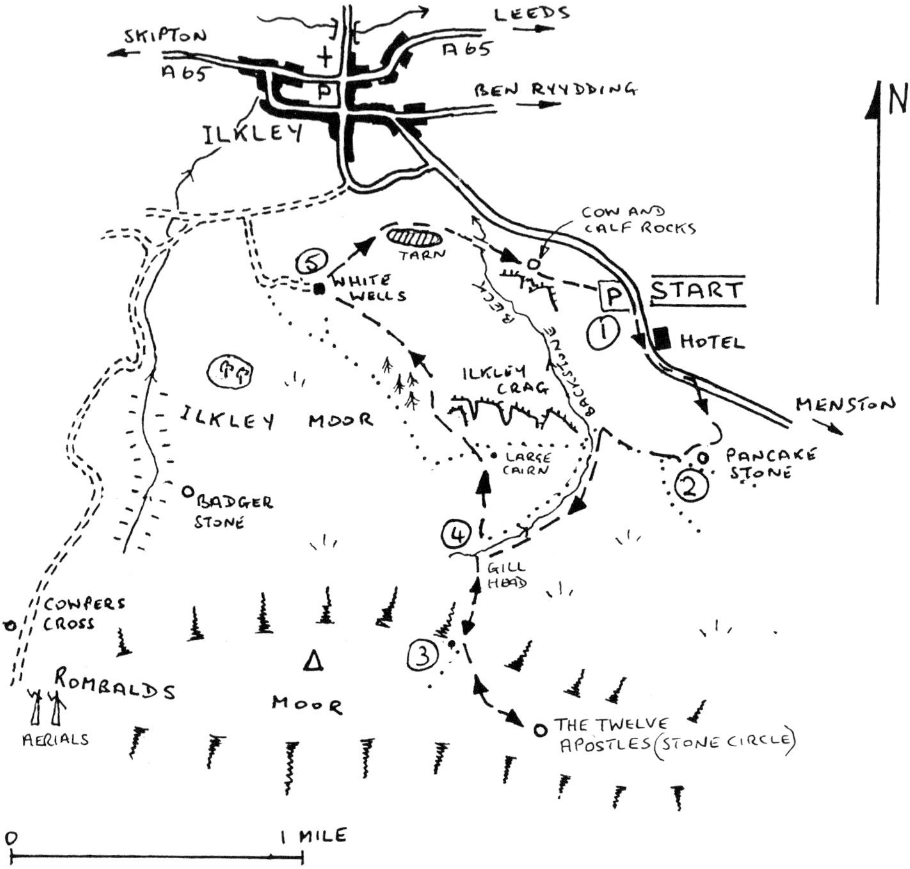

CUP AND RING CARVINGS

Route 8

Ilkley Moor and Twelve Apostles — 4¼ miles

START: *The car park at the Cow and Calf Rocks just outside Ilkley at G.R. SE133467, O.S. Landranger sheet 104 (Leeds and Bradford). Ilkley is located on the A65 15 miles north-west of Leeds and 6 miles north of Bingley.*

ROUTE

1. *From the car park walk up the road beyond the Cow and Calf Hotel then veer right up a track ascending to the Pancake Stone on the skyline.*
2. *Turn right and follow a level path, passing a large boulder, to where it turns sharp left at Backstone Beck. Walk parallel with the beck for ½ mile then turn left and follow a boardwalk footpath for ½ mile to the boundary stone on the ridge.*
3. *Turn left here and follow a path to the Twelve Apostles stone circle. Return to the boundary stone and back down the board walk to Gill Head.*
4. *Cross the stream and climb the far bank to follow the obvious path to a large cairn on the scarp edge. Descend beside Ilkley Crag and trace the path to White Wells.*
5. *Take the path descending on the right side of bath house, and keeping a pond on your right. Head for a pyramid shaped boulder ahead, then follow the path down to the tarn. Follow the path along the left edge of the tarn to the continuing path at the far side. This climbs the fellside, crossing Backstone Beck at a footbridge, then continues to Cow and Calf Rocks and the car park.*

ACCESS BY BUS/TRAIN

Regular rail services from Leeds and Bradford with connections from other centres. Yorkshire Rider bus, No. 650 from Bradford; 733, 734, 739 from Leeds.

From the cairn a path descends steeply to the old bath house at White Wells. Here in a whitewashed building can be seen the original cold water plunge pool. This represents a forerunner of the spa movement, built in the 1760's by Squire Middleton.

The returning route passes The Tarn complete with ducks, then climbs gradually towards the Cow and Calf and the starting point.

Refreshments Kiosk at the Cow and Calf Rocks car park. The Cow and Calf Hotel serves children's meals.

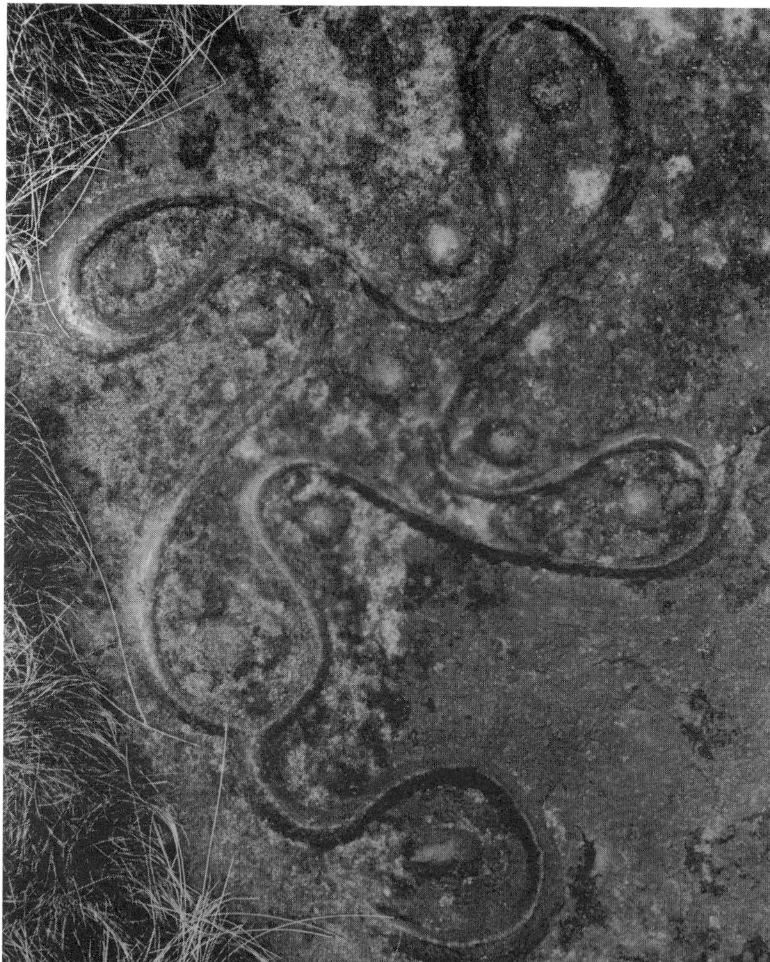

THE SWASTIKA STONE

Route 9 **6¼ miles**

(shorter variation 5¼ miles)

The Swastika Stone

Outline Ilkley—Swastika Stone—Netherwood House—River Wharfe—Old Bridge—Manor House—Ilkley

Shorter Variation Ilkley—Swastika Stone—Panorama Rocks—Canker Well—Ilkley

Summary Plenty of interesting rock formations and legends of giants to fire the young imagination and keep the adult guessing at the purpose of these strange carvings. Good paths on the outward journey trace edge of moors, giving extensive vistas which contrast with idyllic riverside scenery on the return. As well as moorland scenery, Ilkley itself has a considerable pedigree. Here are mineral springs, museums, Viking remains and the traces of a Roman fort.

Attractions Starting and finishing in Ilkley gives the reader the option of enjoying the many delights of the town before or after the walk. The town stands at an important cross-roads and the site of the Roman fort of Olicana, part of which is occupied today by the central car park.

Much of the Victorian splendour of this former spa town is still reflected in its fine architecture, the Arcade, Riverside Gardens and The Grove. Beginning with a stroll along the leafy Mill Ghyll with its babbling brook spanned by petite bridges, the high moors beckon.

Good pathways depart from the top of town and, heading west, gently climb towards Woodhouse Crag. Although the altitude is a mere 900ft the view is superb, a significant factor, perhaps, in the siting of the nearby Swastika Stone. Iron railings protect this Bronze Age rock carving from the careless tramping of walkers' boots.

This artifact is a composite arrangement of five cups and spiralling arms suggestive of a cross more in the imagination than reality. The carving is the only one of its kind in Britain, though similar stones exist in Italy and Sweden.

Leaving the mystifying Swastika Stone, level walking along what may be a track of prehistoric origins, eventually descends towards Addingham Moorside where a choice of return route presents itself. On the one hand field paths and the riverside Dales Way pass the Old bridge, remains of the Roman fort and the Manor House Museum, the second entering town by way of the Panorama Rocks and the picturesque Canker Well Gardens.

Panorama Rocks is a fine example of cup and ring carvings, while the

continued on page 44

Route 9

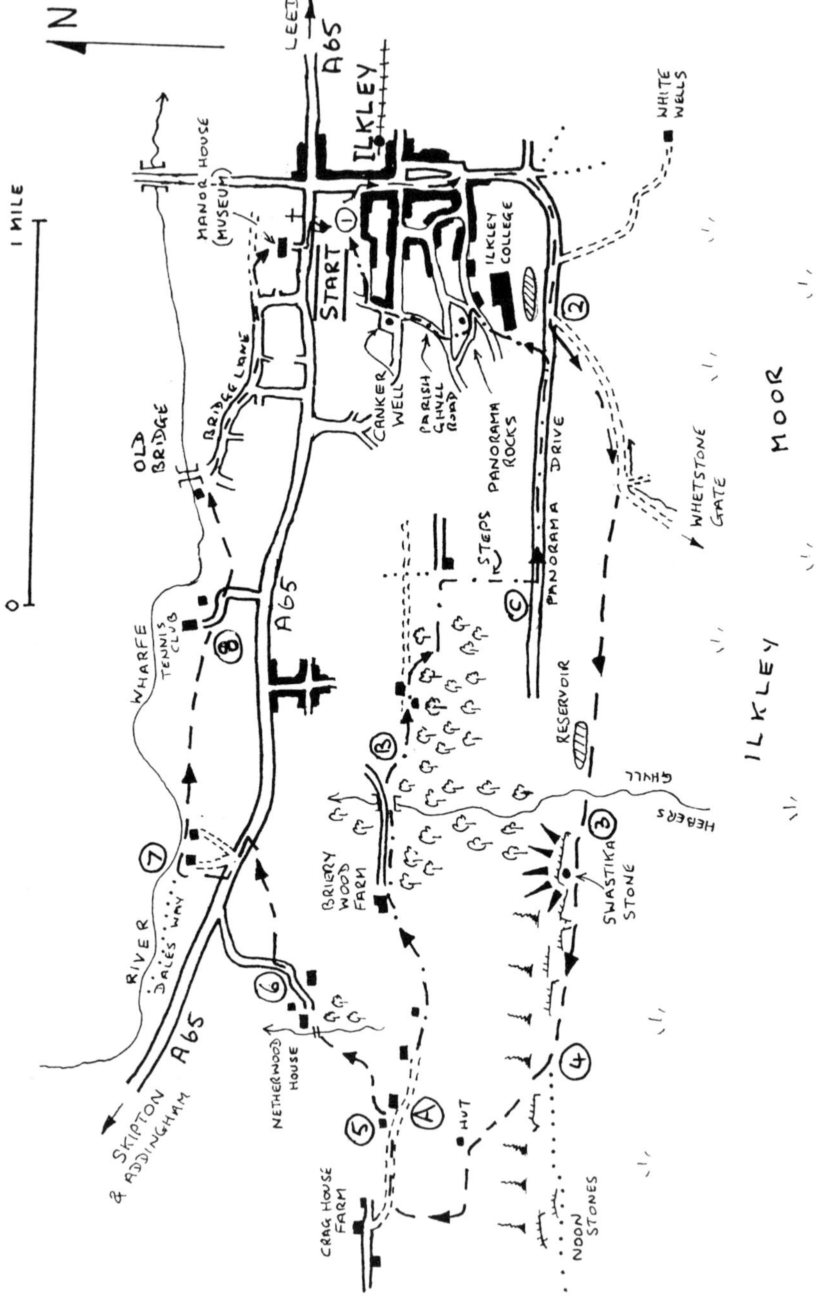
N
1 MILE
0
LEEDS
A65
ILKLEY
WHITE WELLS
MANOR HOUSE (MUSEUM)
START
1
ILKLEY COLLEGE
2
CANKER WELL
PARISH GHYLL ROAD
PANORAMA ROCKS
BRIDGE LANE
OLD BRIDGE
ILKLEY MOOR
WHETSTONE GATE
STEPS
C
PANORAMA DRIVE
A65
TENNIS CLUB
8
WHARFE
RESERVOIR
B
HEBERS GHYLL
3
SWASTIKA STONE
BRIERY WOOD FARM
7
RIVER
DALES WAY
6
A65
NETHERWOOD HOUSE
4
A
5
HUT
SKIPTON & ADDINGHAM
CRAG HOUSE FARM
NOON STONES

Parts 1-3 15/10/95
≃ 2 hrs Mich, Matt & me.

Route 9

The Swastika Stone — 6¼ miles

(shorter variation 5¼ miles)

START: *Ilkley on the A65. Town centre car park off Church Street. G.R. SE117478, O.S. Landranger sheet 104 (Leeds and Bradford).*

ROUTE

1. *From the east exit of the car park turn right up Brook Street and walk along Mill Ghyll beside Wells Promenade. Turn left and left again into Wells Road following this around to the right.*
2. *Just beyond Ilkley College turn left up an ascending metalled track. Where this bends sharp left take the path forward. Pass a small reservoir and after ½ mile reach the railing protecting the Swastika Stone.*
3. *To continue, follow the obvious path, crossing six stiles. Shortly after passing a cairn on your left, another stile is crossed.*
4. *Just a few yards ahead the path angles right, down through boulders towards a hut by a wall. Turn left and follow the wall to reach and cross a gap stile. Walk downhill and turn right along a track. Go as far as next farm.*
5. *Turn left into the wall corner just before the house and cross a stile. Following power lines, a path leads to a fence at the far side. Go through a gate and continue in the same direction downhill, passing a wall corner, then head for Netherwood House. Go through a gate and along a drive beyond the houses to a sharp bend. Turn left down the lane, looking for a stile on the right where the iron railings end.*
6. *Turn right and walk along a hedge and through a stile and a hole in the ruined wall beyond. Head downhill for the bottom right corner of the field by a stream. Go through a gate and walk parallel with the stream. Turn right through the next gate and stride across the stream, turning left for the bottom right corner of field. Go through a gate and follow the edge of the following two fields to reach the A65. Turn left through a gate and cross the road to a driveway. Go through a gate and continue along the right side of a field to reach another gate.*
7. *After this cross a footbridge and turn right along the river bank. Cross a second bridge and go through an iron gate. With a fence on your right, follow a line of trees to a kissing gate. Bear right between two beech trees and continue along fence to a gate at 180 yards. Cross the next pasture to a gate, then continue alongside a hawthorn hedge, veering slightly right at a sign on a tall ash tree to reach yet another gate. Walk towards a line*

of trees and pass through a gate leading onto a metalled lane by the tennis club.

8. *Walk to the right and, at a right hand bend, turn left along a riverside path to emerge by the Old Bridge. Continue straight forward into Bridge Lane and, at its junction with Lister Street, take the dirt road dead ahead. A ¼ mile further on turn right towards the rear of the Manor House Museum, passing the remains of a Roman wall. Walk down the left side of the museum into a yard and through an archway into Church Street. Turn left then right to return to the car park.*

Shorter Variation

As for 1 to 5 above, then:

A. Walk forward through the gate by Hardwick House Farm and at the next farm bear ½ right out of the yard for 10 yards to a stile. Cross this, turn sharp left to a stile in a wall corner, then follow the obvious path downhill to Brierywood Farm. Go through a gate, walking forward into a drive. 30 yards ahead bear right into woods. Follow the path parallel to the lane, joining this at Hebers Ghyll.

B. Just beyond the bridge climb the steps to the right and trace a path left to the driveway passing Westwood Cottage. Not far beyond Lowmoor Lodge turn right along a track angling up into woods. When a house is met turn right and climb a flight of steps.

C. Turn left down Panorama Drive. Just before Ilkley College turn left down a footpath into Queens Road, turning right to St. Margaret's Church. Cross the road to the Panorama Rocks. Turn left along Princess Road, then first right, down a footpath to a junction. Walk along Parish Ghyll Road, passing the Canker Well Garden into Cunliffe Road. Turn right into the central car park.

ACCESS BY BUS/TRAIN

Regular rail services from Leeds and Bradford with connections from other centres. Yorkshire Rider bus No. 650 from Bradford, 733, 734, 739 from Leeds.

Canker Well Garden is a leafy haven on the site of one of the town's oldest mineral springs. Whichever route is chosen back into town there is plenty of places for clambering on rocks, dabbling in water, bird watching or simply dallying amid countryside at its finest.

Refreshments Several pubs, cafes and tearooms in Ilkley.

Route 10 **6½ miles**

Chevin Forest Park

Outline East Chevin Road (car park)—Forest Park—Pool Bank—East Busk Lane—White Bridge—Wharfemeadows Park—Otley Town—Beacon Hill—White House Visitor Centre—East Chevin Road (car park)

Summary The Chevin Forest Park overlooks Otley town and covers 700 acres of heather uplands and afforestation. This is adequately served by well maintained tracks and bridleways that form part of a circular route along the Chevin, returning along valley bottom paths to Otley and via Beacon Hill.

Attractions One of the principal attractions is the rock formations. The millstone grit outcropping here gains its name from the fact that it was once quarried for use as grinding stones in grain mills. Today rock climbers find the friction and reliability of handholds reassuring. On fine days crag rats (rock gymnasts) may be seen training on boulder problems at Caley Crags. There is a profusion of smaller rocks on which the children can find adventure. See if they can find the Rocking Stone.

The Chevin provides interesting walking amid mixed woods that once formed a deer park owned by the Fawkes family of Farnley Hall, Otley. In 1946 Major Horton Fawkes gave 263 acres of the land to the town of Otley. Since then Leeds City Council acquired the land and made additions. The forest park consists of planted softwoods amid older mixed woodland and open heathlands in which plants and wildlife abounds.

There is a magnificent view from The Chevin at Beacon Hill, dominated in the foreground by the jutting prow of Great Almscliff Crag. Further afield, on clear days, can be seen York Minster, the White Horse of Kilburn, Beamsley Beacon and Great Whernside. The charm and beauty of the area caught the imagination of that itinerant 19th century artist J. M. W. Turner who produced several works featuring the Chevin and its open vistas.

After traversing across the Chevin and negotiating level going along the valley bottom pastures Mum and Dad can take in the rural charm of Otley with its popular outdoor market, bric-à-brac shops, etc. The chance to browse and marshal available strength for the climb up to Beacon Hill before returning to the car.

Refreshments The White House Visitor Centre has an adjoining tea room. Various pubs and cafes in Otley.

Route 10

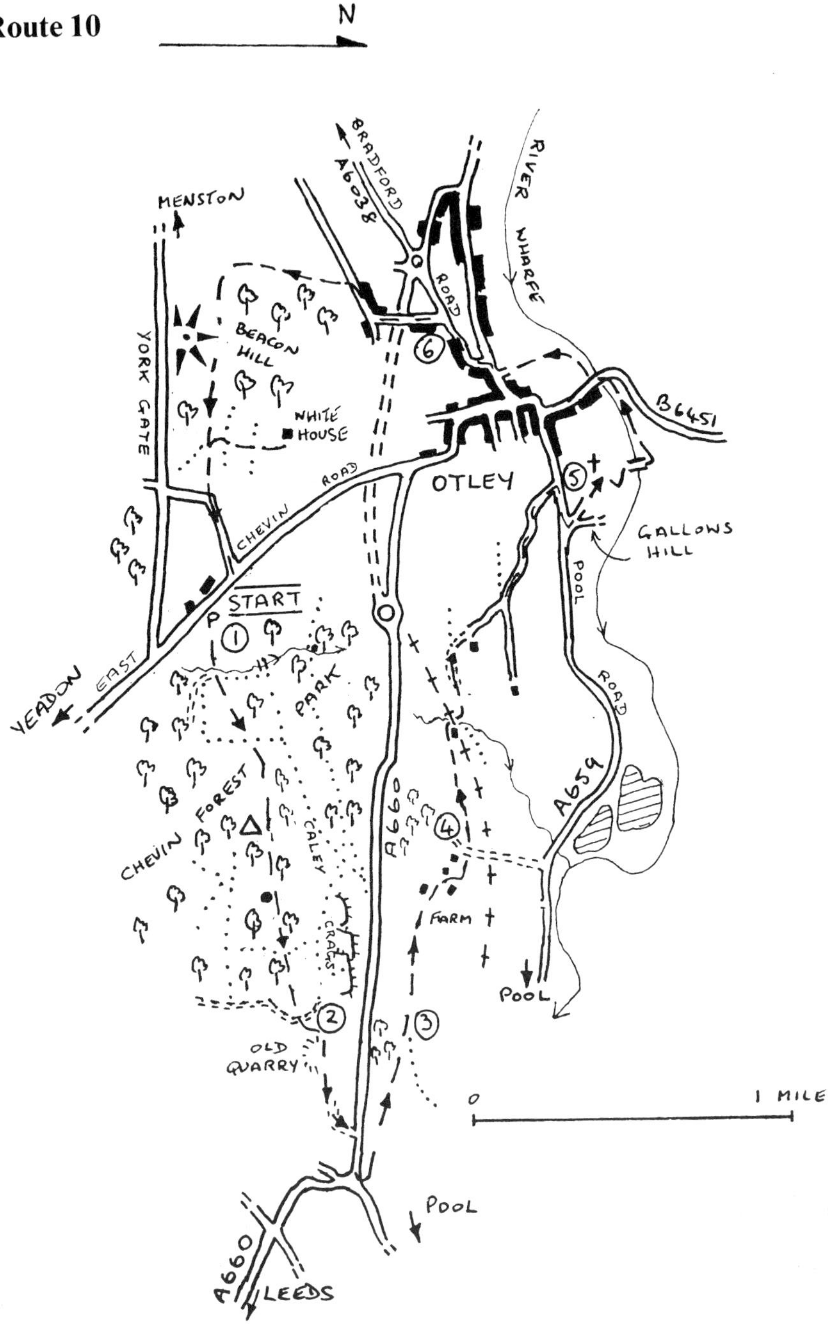
N
BRADFORD
A6038
RIVER WHARFE
MENSTON
ROAD
YORK GATE
BEACON HILL
WHITE HOUSE
6
B6451
CHEVIN ROAD
OTLEY
5
GALLOWS HILL
POOL ROAD
START
P
1
EAST
YEADON
PARK
CHEVIN FOREST
CALEY
A660
4
A659
FARM
CRAGS
POOL
2
3
OLD QUARRY
0
1 MILE
POOL
A660
LEEDS

Route 10

Chevin Forest Park 6½ miles

START: *At the car park located just off the East Chevin Road 1½ miles from Otley town centre and just beyond the junction with Miller Lane. G.R. SE217443. Otley is located at the junction of the A659 and A660 10 miles from Leeds. O.S. Landranger sheet 104 (Leeds and Bradford) or Stile Map for Chevin area.*

ROUTE

1. *Leave the car park at its east side and follow a track parallel to the dale. After crossing a small brook this contours around hill below a triangulation pillar, passing a memorial stone to meet a junction of paths.*
2. *Carry straight on to the edge of the trees and turn left along a bridleway, then walk to the right around the bottom of a disused quarry to meet the A660. Turn right along the road and first left at old Pool Bank. On the corner itself turn left through a stile and follow a field path below a wood to join a path from the right.*
3. *Continue forward for ¼ mile and cross a stile. Veer right in front of a building, through a gate and continue forward to Caley Hall Farm, bearing to the right to reach a stile in the wall. Turn left through this and follow the path along a field boundary to cut across a track.*
4. *A field path continues to a farmhouse. Between this and the tunnel beneath the railway turn right through a gate and walk over the embankment, descending to a hedge. Walk left, following a path leading into East Busk Lane and walk ¾ mile along this to Pool Road.*
5. *Turn right, then first left at Gallows Hill. Bear left immediately to a gate. Follow the path to the left of the gate, following it to White Bridge. Cross this and turn left along the riverbank to reach a main road. Turn left to cross the bridge then right along a riverside path, continuing around to the left to meet the A660 Ilkley Road. Turn right, then left up Bradford Road.*
6. *Not far ahead turn up West Chevin Road, continue over the bypass and around to the right. Cross the first stile on the left and climb steeply through a gate. When the next field boundary is reached, ignore the stile and, instead walk left for ½ mile beneath Beacon Hill to a junction of paths. The left branch descends to the White House but, by continuing*

forward through two gates, Miller Lane is entered and followed to a 'T' junction. Turn right to return to the starting point.

ACCESS BY BUS

Yorkshire Rider Service 784 from Leeds.

UNITED REFORMED CHURCH, SALTAIRE

Route 11 **3¾ miles**

(shorter variation 2½ miles)

Shipley Glen and Tramway

Outline Hirst Lane Picnic Site—Canal Towpath—Saltaire—Roberts Park—Glen Railway—Bracken Hall—Dowley Gap Aqueduct—Canal Towpath—Hirst Lane Picnic Site.

Summary An interesting circuit taking in the Bracken Hall Countryside Centre and linking canal towpath, bridleways and riverbank. All the walking is easy with distant views. A waterbus, a Victorian inclined cable railway and fun park are just some of the diversions which will transform this route into a memorable day outing all within the space of a little less than 4 miles.

Attractions This walk is singular in its tremendous variety, fine landscape blended with a lingering legacy of West Riding industrial heritage. Leaving a canal side picnic site the walk starts with a towpath stroll into Saltaire, a model village mostly off route but worthy of the diversion to inspect its fine buildings.

It was the brainchild of Sir Titus Salt, son of an early 19th century wool merchant who built a mill and then provided a complete village catering for his employees every need, except that is, for a pub! The architecture reflects Italian flamboyance, the mill chimney to the north of the canal for instance, being modelled in the manner of the campanile at the church of Santa Maria Gloriosa in Venice. The mill now houses various units, including the 1853 gallery which houses works by the Bradford photographer David Hockney.

Immediately opposite the mill is the United Free Church, built in the Roman Classic style. Further up Victoria road is the Saltaire Institute complete with stone lions originally destined for London's Trafalgar Square. Even further up the way are some fine alms houses and the Titus Salt Hospital, visited in 1871 by Charles Dickens junior.

From Saltaire pathways cross the river (**rowing boats for hire**) into Roberts Park then climb to Shipley Glen. The younger ramblers will probably prefer to take the novel way up by way of the cable tramway. At the top is a small fun fair and short stroll to Bracken Hall Visitor Centre on the flanks of Shipley Glen.

From across the dale the famous ravine appears like a verdant gash that has bitten deep into the plateau dividing Gilstead Moor from that of Baildon. Prehistoric querns found here testify to habitation by early man. The countryside centre is a focal point for nature trails and exhibits featuring local wildlife and natural history.

continued on page 52

Route 11

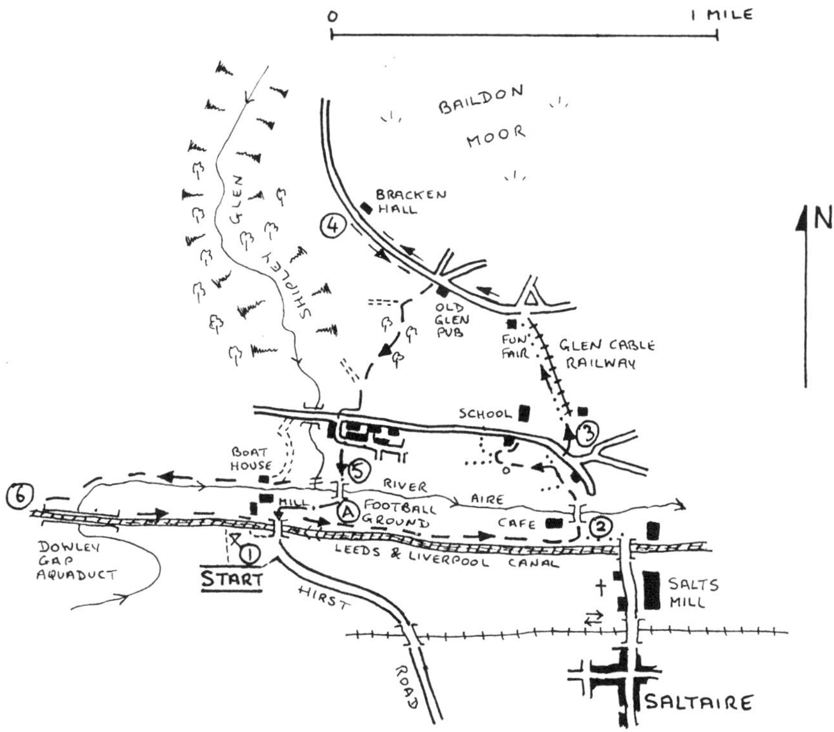

0
1 MILE
BAILDON
MOOR
N
BRACKEN HALL
SHIPLEY GLEN
OLD GLEN PUB
FUN FAIR
GLEN CABLE RAILWAY
SCHOOL
BOAT HOUSE
RIVER AIRE
MILL
FOOTBALL GROUND
CAFE
DOWLEY GAP AQUADUCT
START
LEEDS & LIVERPOOL CANAL
HIRST ROAD
SALTS MILL
SALTAIRE

Route 11

Shipley Glen and Tramway — 3¾ miles

(shorter variation 2½ miles)

START: *The car park and picnic site in Hirst Lane, G.R. SE130383, O.S. Landranger sheet 104 (Leeds and Bradford). Reached from the roundabout at the junction of the A657 and the A650 at Saltaire.*

ROUTE

1. *From the car park cross the canal bridge and turn right, following the towpath for ½ mile to Saltaire bridge.*
2. *Turn left, passing the boathouse and crossing a footbridge over the river to Roberts Park. Walk forward passing a house on your right, then take next left to Sir Titus Salt statue. Follow the path to the right and, just after a shelter, turn left into Coach Road and walk right to a footpath (**sign to Glen Railway and The Glen**).*
3. *Turn left to the railway. If not operating, follow the path ascending on its left, and at Prod Lane continue ahead to the junction by the Old Glen tea room. Walk forward 150 yards to Bracken Hall Countryside Centre.*
4. *Return to the Old Glen and turn right just before this. Follow a bridleway downhill, ignoring all branches, to reach the road. Turn right, then left along Glenwood Avenue. Immediately after 4th block of flats on your right, turn right on a path (**Rydal Avenue**).*
5. *At the corner bear right towards the river. Turn right to cross a footbridge over the stream. Walk along a dirt road, between buildings, and with the rowing club on your right follow the riverbank to Dowley Gap.*
6. *Turn left along the canal and follow this to the Hirst Lane canal bridge ½ mile distant. Turn right over the bridge to start.*

Shorter Variation

A. As for 1 to 5 above, but instead of turning right walk straight ahead and cross footbridge over the River Aire. Bear right toward mill, then left across the canal bridge to the car park.

ACCESS BY BUS/TRAIN

Metro trains link Leeds and Bradford with Saltaire. Keighley and District bus services 666/667 from Bradford. A waterbus service (**in season**) operates between Shipley and Bingley, stopping at Hirst Lane locks and Saltaire bridge.

Refreshments may be taken at the Glen tearoom while the children clamber about on nearby rocks. Continuing the walk, a descending bridleway returns to the valley for easy level walking along the riverbank to the seven arch Dowley Gap aqueduct. Children who didn't know watercourses could cross each other can see the Aire flowing beneath the Leeds and Liverpool canal on its way to the North Sea. Continuing stretches alongside the canal then return to the start.

Refreshments The Old Glen pub and tea rooms at Shipley Glen. Saltaire boat house operates a cafe during summer.

NORTHCLIFF WOODS

Route 12 **2½ miles**

Northcliff Woods

Outline Cliff Gardens—Northcliff Woods—Heaton Shay—Chalybeate Spring—Royds Cliff Wood—Cliff Gardens

Summary A short walk through natural broad leaf woodlands a stones throw from Bradford City centre. As such it provides the welcome if limited 'bolthole' for local residents or an unexpected backwater of natural tranquillity within the city limits, yet again demonstrating the county's green assets.

Attractions This route takes advantage of a finger of mature natural woodland that leafs its way into the Frizinghall and Manningham districts of Bradford suburbia. The mainly oak and beech woodlands support a population of grey squirrels which have almost reached plague proportions, nevertheless children love to watch their acrobatics in the treetops.

There is abundant birdlife too, including sighting of jay, wood pigeon, tree creepers, nuthatches and wrens to mention just a few. An additional diversion is a small gauge steam railway which offers rides to young children on Sundays between May and October.

If it is possible to drag the youngsters away from this sideshow pleasant ascending pathways strike westwards through Northcliff Woods. This is an especial pleasure in autumn when leaves in every shade of gold, brown and yellow lie in deep drifts along the way.

The walk in fact connects two fingers of woodland by a right of way across a golf course. At Heaton Shay a narrow metalled lane is followed through farmland passing the 17th century farmhouse at Heaton Royds. Built into the wall by the road side here is an old water trough by a spring. This bears the inscription J. Field Esquire.

The road is followed into a dell where a path leads off left into the more interesting route through Royds Cliff Woods. The path follows Red Beck which derives its name from a chalybeate spring where a strong flow of iron rich water bubbles to the surface.

The well figures in a local legend as well as furnishing the city coat of arms and crest featuring a pigs head. Apparently a wild boar roamed the woods terrorising local inhabitants. A magistrate offered a reward for the man who killed the beast. A hunter waited by the spring where the pig often drank. Successfully killing it the hunter ripped out the pig's tongue and set off to collect his reward.

Another man meanwhile, found the dead pig and returned with the

continued on page 56

Route 12

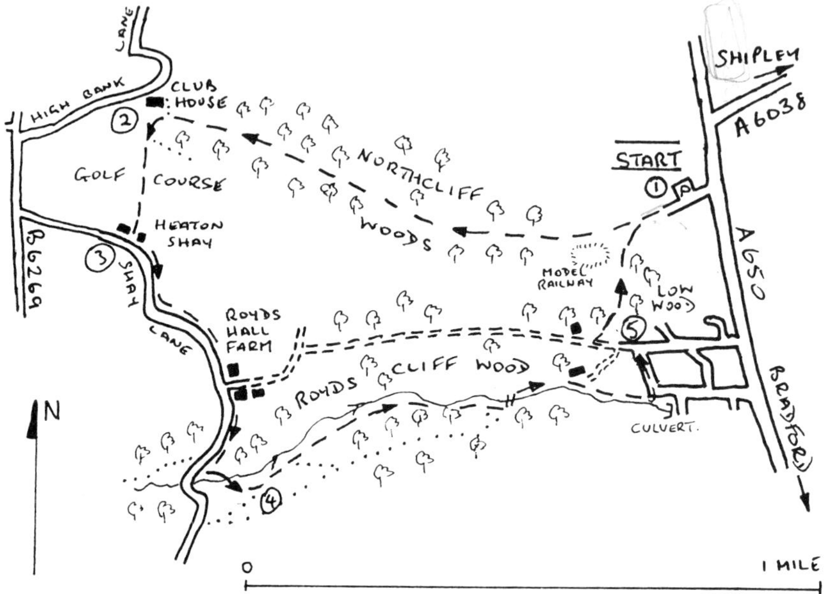

ENGLISH OAK

Route 12

Northcliff Woods 2½ miles

START: *Car parking in Cliff Wood Avenue adjacent to Cliff Gardens just off the A650 close to its juction with the A6038 at Shipley. G.R. SE145366, O.S. Landranger sheet 104 (Leeds and Bradford).*

ROUTE

1. *From the car park in Cliff Gardens walk along the tarmac path into the woods. A dirt track continues past a miniature gauge railway track and ascends steadily for one mile.*
2. *Climb the steps to your left to reach a wall corner. Ignore the path going left here and continue alongside the wall across the golf course (**care**) to reach a gap stile. Go through this and follow a path between houses to Shay Lane.*
3. *Turn left and walk along the road, winding downhill to a stream. Turn left through a gap in the wall and cross the stream at the stepping stones.*
4. *Bear left along an obvious path into the Woods. After crossing Red Beck for the last time the path ascends the bank then bears right past some garages to Wilmer Drive. Turn left, then left again (**Redburn Drive**) to reach the entrance to Heaton Royds School.*
5. *Walk forward up a stony track then pick up a path to the right going through Low Wood. A bouldery trail is followed 200 yards before descending into Northcliff Wood, adjacent to the miniature railway. Turn right to return to the car.*

ACCESS BY BUS

Keighley and District bus services 666 and 667 from Bradford interchange.

head also for the reward. The man could offer no account why the head had no tongue, but then the true slayer of the beast appeared with the tongue and received his reward.

About ¾ mile beyond the well the trail rejoins the outward bound route and returns to the start.

Refreshments There are no refreshments on route, the Junction is the nearest pub.

CALVERLEY WOODS

Route 13 **6 miles**

Calverley Woods

Outline Dawson's Corner—Shell Lane—Calverley Woods—West Wood—Ravencliffe Wood—The Blue Pig—Dawson's Corner.

Summary At least half this route forms a woodland trail, the remainder along bridleways and good paths which in part trace the Leeds Country Way. This takes the rambler through the green corridor sandwiched between the conurbations of Bradford and Leeds and provides easy, almost level going throughout.

Attractions Once again a route which will appeal to those with a love of the arboreal delights of the English countryside, and the squirrels that go along with it. The walk passes quite close to the Leeds to Liverpool canal but doesn't actually follow the towpath.

Beginning from Dawsons Corner on the Leeds outer ring road at Pudsey, this walk initially follows bridleways across agricultural land, then descends Shell Lane, a leafy tunnel into the village of Calverley. A brief stroll along the road passes Well Gardens where an old well trough has been incorporated into a rockery.

Calverley is an ancient village and indeed was mentioned in the Domesday survey conducted by the Normans in 1086. It was then recorded as Caverleia and was in the ownership of Arnketill. Calverley Hall now restored, still retains its 15th century roof and is regarded as the finest surviving example of a medieval manor house in the county. It was here in 1604 that Walter Calverley murdered his two sons while in a drunken rage. He was later tried and executed in York.

Just by the parish church a lane leads to South Lodge and the start of Calverley Woods which extend northwards into the alluvial pastures of the Aire Valley. It is said that at night the ghost of squire Calverley can be seen galloping on a headless horse through the trees. Don't leave it too late for this walk!

Despite its obvious antiquity Calverley seems to have been bypassed during the Industrial Revolution. There was a short history of textile working as well as an equally brief fame as a spa. The waters from the spring were said to smell like a polecat!

Leaving South Lodge the pathway through the woodlands describes a semicircular course for over one mile, emerging at the busy A657 at Greengates. Oak woods continue from here along the line of the boundary separating Leeds from Bradford, in fact followed by the Leeds Country Way

continued on page 60

Route 13

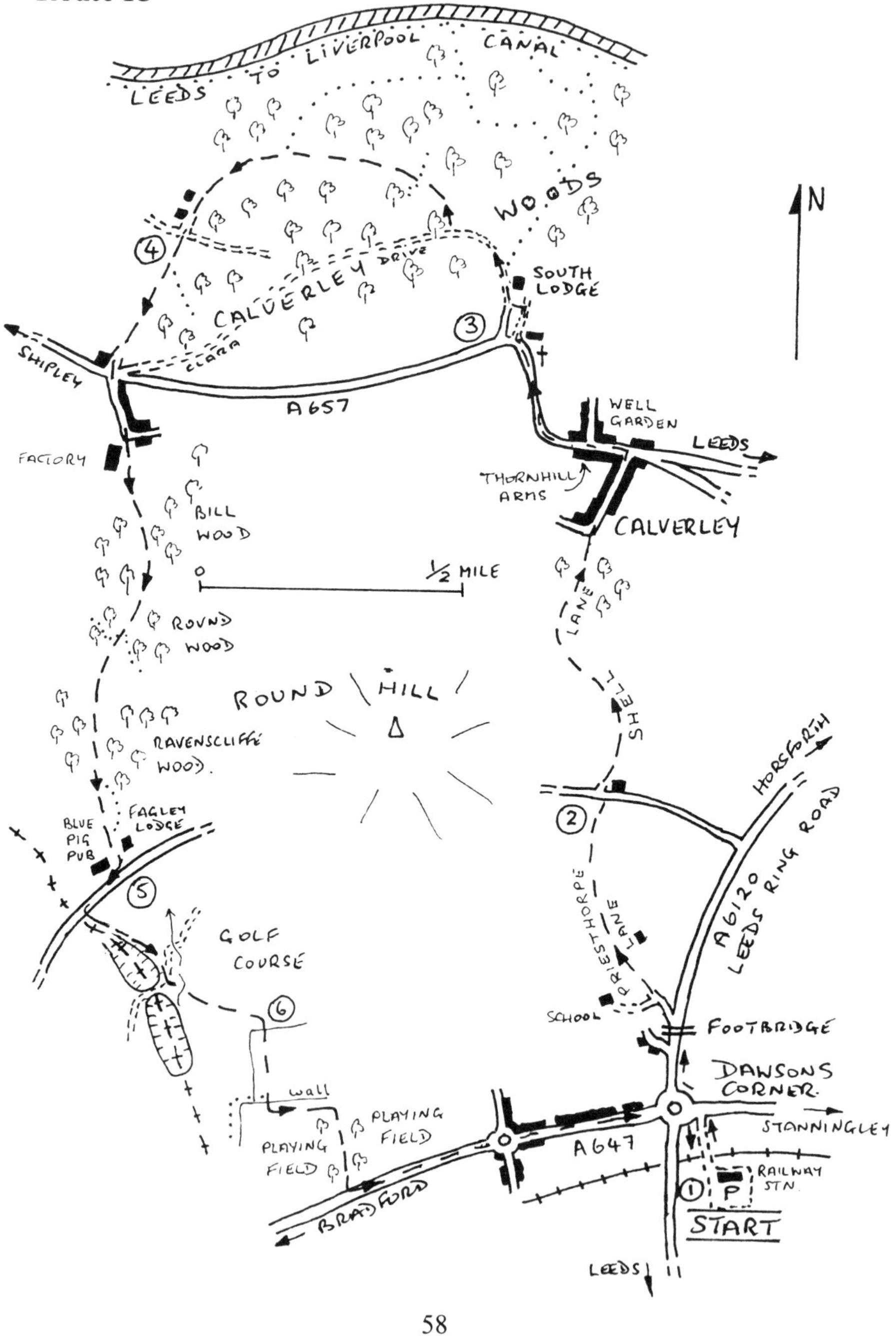

LEEDS TO LIVERPOOL CANAL
WOODS
N
CALVERLEY DRIVE
CALVERLEY
CLARA
SOUTH LODGE
SHIPLEY
A657
WELL GARDEN
LEEDS
FACTORY
THORNHILL ARMS
CALVERLEY
BILL WOOD
0
½ MILE
LANE
ROUND WOOD
ROUND HILL
SHELL
HORSFORTH
RAVENSCLIFFE WOOD.
A6120 LEEDS RING ROAD
BLUE PIG PUB
FAGLEY LODGE
PRIESTHORPE LANE
GOLF COURSE
SCHOOL
FOOTBRIDGE
DAWSONS CORNER
wall
PLAYING FIELD
PLAYING FIELD
STANNINGLEY
A647
RAILWAY STN
P
START
BRADFORD
LEEDS

Route 13

Calverley Woods 6 miles

START: *Car parking at New Pudsey railway station at Dawson's Corner, G.R. SE211343. O.S. Landranger sheet 104 (Leeds and Bradford). Alternative, park at start of Priesthorpe Lane.*

ROUTE

1. *Take the exit from the station car park, turning left to the roundabout, then right along the ring road to the footbridge. Cross this and just beyond, bear left past the school gate into Priesthorpe Lane, following this to a 'T' junction after ¾ mile.*
2. *Turn left then right down a bridleway* ***(Shell Lane).*** *This wends its way eventually to Monson Avenue. Walk down this to the A657. Cross the road and turn left past the Well Garden and continue along the road to an acute left bend by the church.*
3. *Walk down the lane* ***(signed The Barn)*** *left of some mews cottages to a gate. Bear left into a driveway and right to South Lodge. Follow the metalled lane for 100 yards and turn right to a gate and a stile. Go through this and follow the woodland track for one mile to a gate with a large house on your right. Continue straight forward to a sharp right bend.*
4. *Walk through the gate in the fence ahead and follow the avenue* ***(Eleanor Drive)*** *uphill for ½ mile to a gate. Go through this, cross the A657 and walk along Ravenscliffe Road. Where this turns left as Crowther Avenue, walk forward on a footpath beside a factory, ascending into Bill Wood. Ignoring a gate on your left, pass a clearing to enter Round Wood where the path divides. Take the middle way, ignoring paths left and right. Cross a stile to a gate by Fagley Lodge. Just beyond this a dirt road is met at the Blue Pig pub.*
5. *Bear right towards the disused railway, but just before the dismantled bridge walk left along a track beside the embankment leading to a path beside a fence. At a bridge over the cutting, turn left over a stile and follow a line of power cables across the golf course to a wall corner.*
6. *Go through a gate, turning right alongside a wall to a stile. Go through this and another stile a few yards further on. With a wall on your left initially, continue forward towards trees. Go through a stile and turn right tracing the path back to the A647. Turn left and after ¾ mile reach Dawson's Corner roundabout, then turn right into the station car park.*

ACCESS BY BUS/TRAIN

Metro bus service 71 from Leeds and Ring Road circular service No. 9. There are frequent train services between Leeds and New Pudsey station.

---

long distance path. Just after the Blue Pig pub the dismantled Pudsey to Shipley rail link is crossed and field paths extend to the main A647 Bradford road and shortly afterwards the return to Dawson's Corner.

Refreshments Thornhill Arms, Calverley (outside tables) and the Blue Pig, Fagley (children's room provided).

FORGE LOCKS

Route 14 **5¼ miles**

(shorter variation 4 miles)

Kirkstall Valley

Outline Rodley—Canal towpath—River Aire—Newlay Locks—Forge Locks—Bramley Fall—Newlay—Canal towpath—Rodley.

Summary Predominantly a waterside walk along the Leeds and Liverpool Canal, but with a stretch by the river Aire. The route may be extended if desired with an additional 1¼ miles taking in Bramley Fall Woods. Unless this longer route is taken the route will be entirely without climbing.

Attractions This walk offers the contrasting landscape of riverside scenery and one reflecting the heyday of the Industrial Heritage of the old West Riding. Along the inland waterway are converted mills and a chance to see canal engineering in action at two sets of locks.

The walk forms a small part of the more extensive Leeds Museums Trail set in the Kirkstall Valley Park. This was established in 1982 to promote the rural beauty of the green wedge of country extending from Calverley, practically to the canal basin in Leeds centre.

The walk is not difficult even if the option through Bramley Fall is taken. Initially following the canal west out of Rodley a change of direction (picnic site here) follows first the river Aire, then the line of the railway. The canal towpath is regained at Newlay where there is quite a busy marina.

One may proceed west here for the straightforward return to the starting point, or as an alternative take in more of the Leeds and Liverpool canal east to Bramley Fall. A circular route from Newlay Locks takes the walker through natural woodlands returning to Forge Locks. From here level walking once again follows the waterway to Newlay and beyond, heading for the start at Rodley.

On route is the Ross Mill Cottage and Ross Valley mill shop. The towpath between Newlay and Rodley is in summer ablaze with wild blooms including vetch, dog rose, elder and buttercups. In places patches of yellow flag are encroaching into the waterway creating habitats for water birds, while the towpath is good blackberrying country in September.

As autumn progresses the overhanging tree cover of willow, silver birch and ash transforms the waterway into a painter's pallette of reflected pastel shades. Rodley itself is a popular venue with young children fishing for tadpoles and tiddlers.

Refreshments The Rodley Barge pub (tables overlooking the canal). The Abbey pub, Newlay (tables outside). Ross Mill Cottage (tea garden, lunches) overlooking river.

Route 14

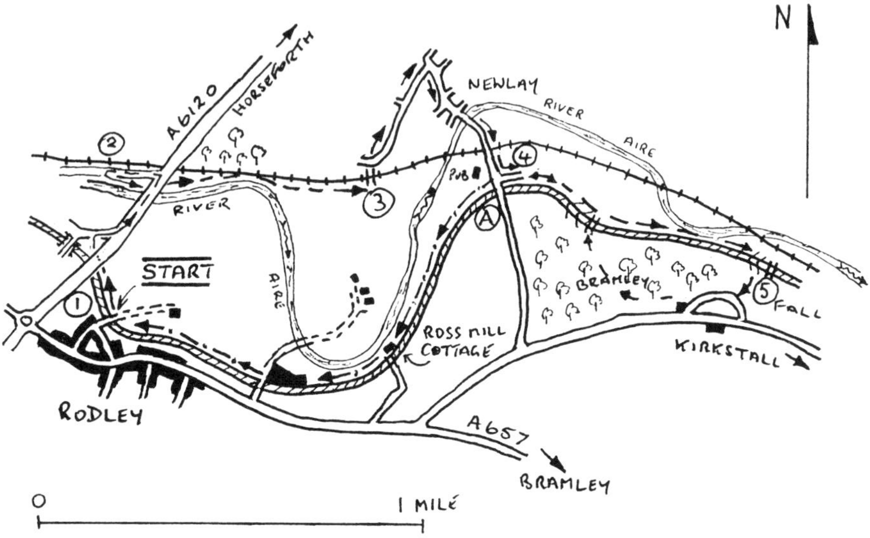

INDIAN BALSAM pink July–Oct

Route 14

Kirkstall Valley

5¼ miles
(shorter variation 4 miles)

START: *Rodley is situated on the A657 close to the junction with the A6120 Leeds Ring Road. Parking in Canal Road or Bridge Road adjacent to the Rodley Barge pub. G.R. SE223365, O.S. Landranger sheet 104 (Leeds and Bradford).*

ROUTE

1. *Cross the swing bridge and turn left alongside the canal, following the towpath beneath the road bridge. Turn immediately right and walk to the main road. Turn left along this, then left down Calverley Lane to a gate after 150 yards.*
2. *Turn left through the gate across the picnic site to the river, then veer left under the road again and proceed downstream alongside Swaine Wood. The obvious path keeps close to the railway line as far as a footbridge.*
3. *Cross this to reach New Laithes Road and turn right along this to the junction with Newlay Lane ¼ mile ahead. Turn downhill across the river and railway to Abbey Pub. Just past this turn left to a gate where a path veers right through a picnic site to the canal.*
4. *Turn left, following the towpath as far as Forge Locks some ¾ mile distant. Turn right over the footbridge.*
5. *Take the steps up into the woods. At the top turn right on a metalled path to reach the park keeper's lodge. Turn right just before this, tracing a woodland trail downhill to rejoin the canal at Newlay Locks. Cross the footbridge and turn left. Follow the towpath for 1¾ miles back to Rodley swing bridge.*

SHORTER VARIATION

As for 1 to 4 above, then:

A. Turn right beneath the bridge and follow the towpath for 1½ miles back to Rodley swing bridge.

ACCESS BY BUS

Keighley and District bus. Service No. 760 from Leeds stops at Rodley.

MORAVIAN SETTLEMENT, FULNECK

Route 15 **4½ miles**

Tong Village and Cockersdale

Outline Sykes Wood—Tong Beck—Tong Village—Keeper Lane—Fulneck Moravian Settlement—Pudsey Beck—Fulneck.

Summary Cockersdale is another of those green oases located in the countryside hemmed in by the sprawling cities of Leeds and Bradford. But don't let this put you off what is undoubtedly a superb walk. This follows well defined woodland paths, tracks and bridleways with some steep uphill bits, especially into Fulneck.

Attractions From the outset the meandering course of Tong Beck is followed along tiny Cockersdale amid mature deciduous woodlands alive with a great variety of bird-life. Plantlife is profuse, the banks of the stream providing abundant beds of Himalayan balsam. Many species of tits may be seen in the woods hereabouts.

After tracing footpaths, which have been partially paved to combat erosion, the bridleway of Springfield Lane climbs towards Tong, a one-street village with a considerable pedigree. It is worth dwelling here for refreshments and to browse.

Tong is mentioned as Tving in the Domesday Book, the record showing that at the time of the survey the thane Steinulfr held four carucates of land under the plough. Centuries later Tong Hall became the home of the Tempests but is now a residential college. Just before this is the village church, standing on foundations dating back to the Dark Ages. By the gate are the village stocks. Fun demonstrations of their purpose can be made by posing in them for photos.

The northwards continuation of the walk leaves the east end of the village by way of Keeper Lane. This represents part of an old packhorse route between Morley and Pudsey. Adjacent to Keeper Lane is the old village pump where water flowed from a lion's mouth. Behind this is the restored site of the village pinfold, a place where stray animals were impounded by a 'pinder' until the owners laid claim to them.

Descending into the Fulneck valley Pudsey Beck leads to a track where the recently lost altitude must now be regained, entering Fulneck, famous for its Moravian settlement and residential school. A brief encounter with a golf course leads to continuing field paths down valley to the start of the walk.

Refreshments The Greyhound Inn, Tong (tables outside). Bankhouse Inn, Fulneck (tables outside).

Route 15

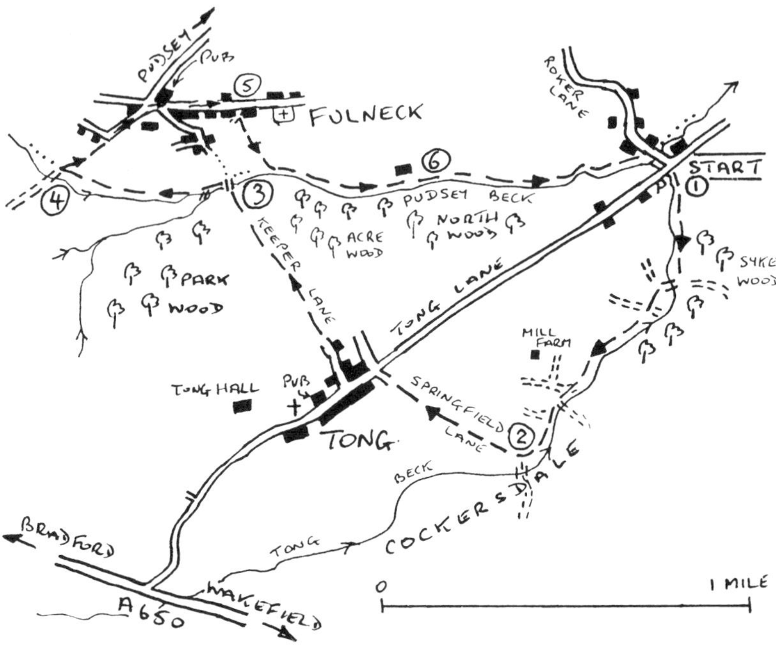

BOUNDARY STONE,
ROMBALD'S MOOR

Route 15

Tong Village and Cockersdale — 4½ miles

START: *The junction of Tong Lane with Roker Lane. There is space for a few cars at the roadside by the entrance to Sykes Wood. G.R. SE237316, O.S. Landranger sheet 104 (Leeds and Bradford).*

ROUTE

1. *From the layby go through two gates, bearing right downhill towards the beck. Follow the obvious pathway left through Sykes Wood to a footbridge. Cross this and climb uphill, veering left to a fence. Cross a stile and continue forward on partially flagged pathway to a parting of the ways 200 yards ahead. Ignore the right branch, walking 25 yards to stile. Cross this and carry straight on cutting across a track to where a second track is joined where this swings right. Continue forward and descend to a fence. Cross the stile and ignore the bridge over the beck. Continue forward* ***(look for posts with yellow arrows)*** *crossing yet another stile within 30 yards, soon afterwards reaching a stile by a gate.*
2. *Go through this and turn right up a stony track as far as Tong Lane. Turn left into the village, then right down Keeper Lane. By the house veer left, descending a bridleway to Pudsey Beck.*
3. *Cross a footbridge and turn left. Then, ignoring a second bridge and path signposted to Fulneck, walk forward between waymarked stone posts. Walk along the fence by the stream as far as a stile. Cross this and follow a field path to a farm track* ***(Scholebrook Lane).***
4. *Go over stile and turn right, climbing uphill to a road junction. Turn right along Bank House and proceed into the Moravian Settlement at Fulneck.*
5. *Just beyond the shop turn right down Diehouse Lane* ***(no sign),*** *following it around to the right. Just before the factory turn left down a bridleway to the golf course. Cross the fairway* ***(beware golf balls!)*** *toward the beck, and turn left to a stile by the green. Cross this and a further stile not far ahead. At the factory pass through another stile and a gap in the wall, walking to your right between the building and the beck side.*
6. *Beyond factory well marked field paths continue along beckside from stile to stile for about ¾ mile to a gate. Go through this and follow the path between buildings to emerge at Roker Lane. Turn right, then right into Tong Lane and return to the car.*

MENAGERIE POND, TEMPLE NEWSAM

Route 16 **3 miles**

Temple Newsam and Home Farm

Outline Car Park—Jacobean Mansion—Dunstan Hills—Avenue Woods—Lakes—Parkland—Home Farm—Stable Court—Car Park.

Summary An excellent route offering an easy half day amble amid picturesque parkland. It is ideal for a hot summer day, with plenty to see and retain the interest of young children and parents alike, from the working rare breeds farm and museum to the Tudor splendour and works of art of Temple Newsam.

Attractions Temple Newsam has sometimes been referred to as the 'Hampton Court of the North' and it is certainly worthy of the title. It was mentioned in the Domesday survey of 1086 as Neuhusu (new houses) and was owned by the Knights Templar.

The present house was built in c. 1500 by Thomas Lord Darcy and subsequently remodelled over the following three centuries. It is set amid 1000 acres of well appointed grounds and parklands. Within the mansion can be seen some fine works by Thomas Chippendale whilst collections of both English and Chinese porcelain vie with paintings from masters like Reynolds, Vasari, Ricci and Guardi.

A circuit of the picturesque parklands follows good paths just briefly entering Avenue Woods before circumnavigating the ornamental ponds. These provide safe habitat for moorhen and other water birds. The return leg of this round walk takes in the former stable block and outbuildings. In these is housed Home Farm and Stable Court.

The former contains a farm museum and operates as a working farm with many rare domestic breeds. There is some 300 head of stock including goats, horses, cattle, pigs, ducks, sheep, and poultry. Complementing the beasts are exhibits featuring farming methods of yesteryear.

Other attractions to make this a memorable family day out include both formal and informal gardens, gift shop and a childrens' adventure playground.

Refreshments A cafe serves snacks and teas in the Stable Court building.

Route 16

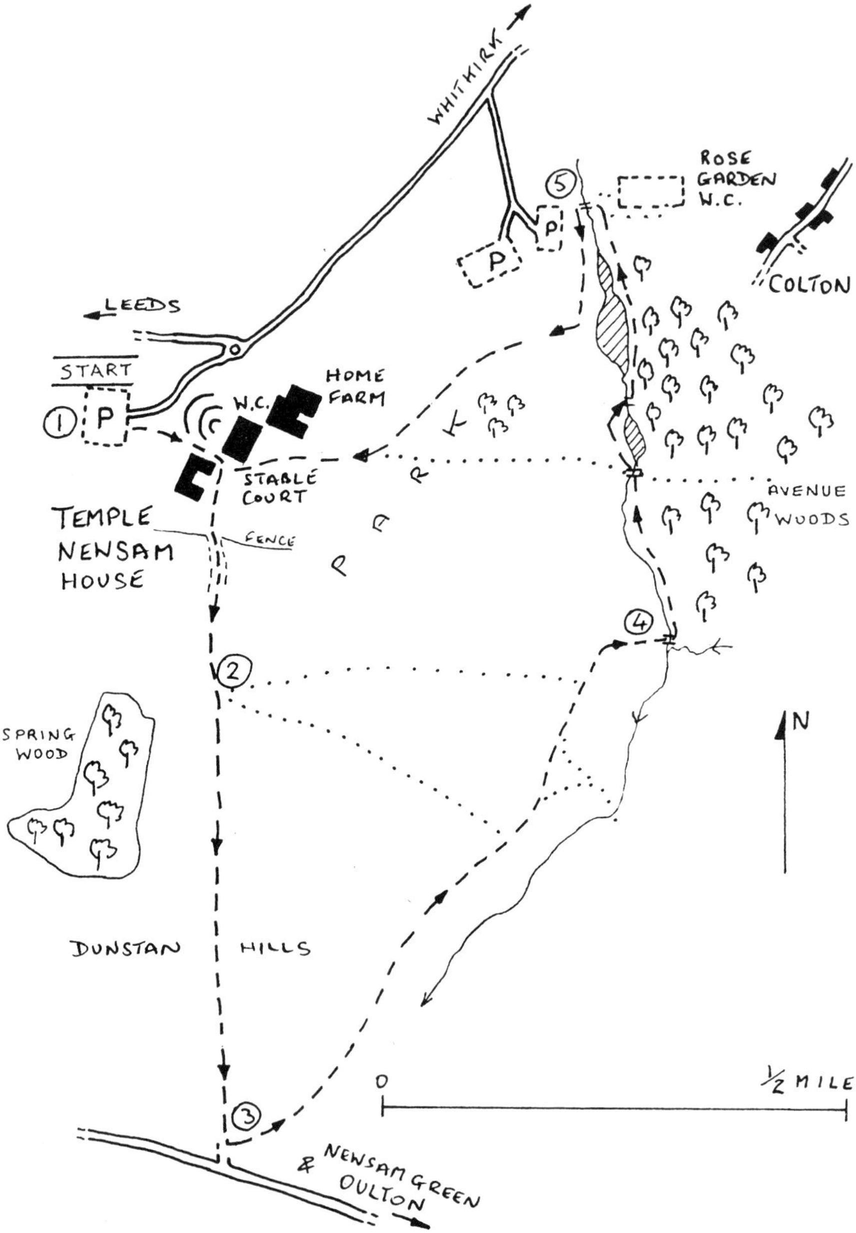
WHITKIRK
LEEDS
START
ROSE GARDEN W.C.
COLTON
HOME FARM
W.C.
STABLE COURT
TEMPLE NEWSAM HOUSE
FENCE
PARK
AVENUE WOODS
SPRING WOOD
N
DUNSTAN HILLS
0
½ MILE
NEWSAM GREEN & OULTON

Route 16

Temple Newsam and Home Farm — 3 miles

START: *Temple Newsam. Access is just off the A63 Leeds to Selby road 5 miles east of the city centre. Car parking adjacent to the manor house. G.R. SE356323, O.S. Landranger sheet 104 (Leeds and Bradford).*

ROUTE

1. *Leave the car park at the east side and walk along the left side of the manor house. Walk around the back of the house and head across a field to a fence. Follow a dirt track to a junction after 60 yards.*
2. *Paths branch off left here, however continue downhill on a tarmac lane to reach a gate on left, just before a new road.*
3. *Turn left along a green track, ignoring paths on both sides. The route bends right into woods to reach a footbridge over a brook.*
4. *Cross this and turn left, shortly re-crossing the stream at a second bridge. Walk to your right, and within yards turn right between Menagerie Ponds, then left along the far bank to a further bridge adjacent to the walled rose garden.*
5. *Turn left over the footbridge and follow a tarmac path across parkland to Home Farm and Stable Court. Continue with these on your right, passing the manor house to regain the car park.*

ACCESS BY BUS

Yorkshire Rider bus service No. 47 from Leeds centre.

SHIPLEY GLEN IN THE SNOW (Route 11)

Appendices

ROUTES IN ORDER OF DIFFICULTY

The walks have been arranged into four categories according to distance, and within each category they are listed in order of difficulty. This is assessed on the basis of how strenuous the walks are relative to each of the other routes in the same category.

Easy short walks (up to 4 miles)

√Route 6—*Harden and Goit Stock Waterfall—3½ miles*
Route 11—*Shipley Glen and Tramway (variation)—2½ miles*
Route 12—*Northcliffe Woods—2½ miles*
Route 16—*Temple Newsam and Home Farm—3 miles*
Route 11—*Shipley Glen and Tramway—3¾ miles*
Route 14—*Kirkstall Valley—4 miles*

More strenuous short walks (4 to 5 miles)

Route 1—*Castle Hill—4 miles*
Route 7—*Bingley and the Druid's Altar—4½ miles*
Route 8—*Ilkley Moor and Twelve Apostles—4½ miles*
Route 15—*Tong Village and Cockersdale—4½ miles*
Route 3—*Stoodley Pike and Rochdale Canal (variation)—4½ miles*

Easy longer walks (5 miles or more)

Route 5—*On the Brontë Trail—7 miles*
Route 10—*Otley Chevin Park—6½ miles*
Route 14—*Kirkstall Valley—5¼ miles*
Route 13—*Calverley Woods—6 miles*
Route 9—*The Swastika Stone (variation)—5¼ miles*

Strenuous walks (5 miles or more)

Route 4—*Crimsworth Dean and Hardcastle Crags—6½ miles*
Route 3—*Stoodley Pike and Rochdale Canal—5½ miles*
Route 9—*The Swastika Stone—6½ miles*
Route 2—*Tunnel End and Standedge—6½ miles*

BUS AND RAIL INFORMATION

Yorkshire Rider. Tel. (0274) 365985
Metro Buses and National Express. Tel. Bradford (0274) 734833
Kirklees Metro. Tel. (0484) 26313
British Rail enquiries. Tel. Leeds (0532) 448133 or Bradford (0274) 733994
A canal waterbus operates between Bingley and Shipley. Tel. (0274) 595914

NATURE RESERVES/TRAILS:

Slurring Rock Nature Trail, Hardcastle Crags, Hebden Bridge.
North Dean Nature Trail, Greetland, Halifax.
Jay Tail Nature Trail, Riddlesden. Two mile circular walk taking in woods, fields and canal towpath on outskirts of Keighley.

Holywell Green Deer Park, Stainland, near Huddersfield. A herd of 400 deer roam parkland crossed by public footpath.
Mark Bottoms Trail, near Holmfirth. Trail taking approx. 1½ hours to complete.
Lotherton Hall Bird Garden. One mile east of A1 near Aberford. Deer Park, woods, gardens and 400 species of colourful birds.
Golden Acre Park, Leeds (6 miles NW of city centre). Comprises 76 acres of woodlands and gardens surrounding a lake. Rock garden, alpine house. Varied plant species and exotic wild fowl.
Tropical World and Canal Gardens, Roundhay Park, Leeds. Aquariums and other living collections of exotic species. Living reconstructions of tropical rain forests.
Lower Spen Bird Sanctuary. 3 hectares of wetland habitat centred upon the River Spen. Located just off the A644 Dewsbury to Mirfield Road at Ravensthorpe.
Bradley Quarry Nature Reserve. At a 5 acre site located just north of the A6107 at Bradley, natural woodland has been allowed to establish itself to form a habitat for many wild flowers and bird species.
Oakwell Hall Country Park, Birstall. Some 87 acres surrounding Oakwell Hall, featured as 'Fieldhead' in Charlotte Brontë's novel 'Shirley'. Tel. (0924) 474926.
Chevin Forest Park, Otley. More than 700 acres of upland heaths, moorlands and woods along the famous Chevin.

WET WEATHER ALTERNATIVES

Museums

The Manor House, Ilkley. Exhibits featuring the region in Roman times. Tel. (0943) 600066
Thwaite Mills, Leeds. 150 years of industrial history revealed in a working watermill set on an island on the river Aire. Tel. (0532) 496453
National Museum of Photography, Bradford. See the science of photography, film and television through exciting exhibits, shows and the unique IMAX big screen cinema. Tel. (0274) 732277.
Industrial Museum, Bradford. Transport and textile machinery housed in former mill. Tel. (0274) 631756
Colour Museum, Bradford. Displays tracing the fascinating story of dyeing. Tel. (0274) 725138.
The Gems and Minerals Museum, Bradford. Collection of gems and rocks from 32 countries. Tel. (0274) 493761.
Tolson Museum, Huddersfield. Features exhibits on local history, transport, textiles, natural science and farming. Tel. (0484) 530591
Colne Valley Museum, Golcar, Huddersfield. Restored weavers' cottages of 1845. Tel. (0484) 659762
Automobilia, Wadsworth, Hebden Bridge. Collection of old cars and motor cycles. Tel. (0422) 844775
City Museum, Leeds. Artifacts and natural history collections from around the world. Tel. (0532) 462465
Abbey House, Kirkstall, Leeds. Folk museum housing period costumes. Central feature a restored Victorian street with shops and cottages. Tel. (0532) 755821
Armley Mills Industrial Museum, Armley, Leeds. Exhibits feature development of industrial Leeds. Includes collection of locomotives. Tel. (0532) 637861
Shibden Hall, Halifax. A fine 15th century building housing a Folk Museum. Tel. (0422) 352246
Horses at Work Museum, Halifax. Tel. (0422) 346835
Bankfield Museum, Halifax. Costume collections. Tel. (0422) 352334

Cliffe Castle, Keighley. Not a castle but a museum and gallery set in parkland with aviary and child's play area. Tel. (0535) 64184

Red House Museum, Gomersal. Charlotte Brontë spent many weekends here. It was used as the model for 'Briarmains' in her novel 'Shirley'. Tel. (0274) 872165

Historic Buildings

East Riddlesden Hall (Nat. Trust), Keighley. Furnished 17th century manor house with adjoining tithe barn. Tel. (0535) 607075

Brontë Parsonage, Haworth. Restored former home of famous Brontë family. Tel. (0535) 42323

Bolling Hall, Bradford. Fine example of Yorkshire manor house reflecting changing domestic needs from 14th century through to 18th century. Tel. (0274) 723057

Piece Hall, Halifax. An 18th century manufacturer's hall featuring arched and colonnaded galleries. Tel. (0422) 68725

White Wells, Ilkley Moor. Original cold water spa bath open to public. Old photographs, displays from town's heyday as a country spa. Tel. The Manor House (0943) 600066.

Kirkstall Abbey, Leeds. Cistercian monastic site founded in 1152

Nostell Priory. An 18th century stately home with a wealth of Chippendale furniture and paintings. Flower gardens and children's adventure playground.

Harewood House. 18th century manor house and bird gardens. Tel. (0532) 886225

Sandal Castle (ruins). Located in the centre of Wakefield, are open to the public with no charge.

Visitor Centres

White House Visitor Centre, Otley Chevin, Otley. Tel. (0943) 465023

Bracken Hall Countryside Centre, Shipley Glen. Tel. (0274) 584140

Tunnel End Countryside Centre, Marsden. Tel. (0484) 846062

Steam Railways

Keighley and Worth Valley Railway. Steam locos ply five miles of preserved track linking Keighley with stations at Ingrow West, Damens, Oakworth, Haworth and Oxenhope. Tel. (0535) 45214.

Middleton Railway, Leeds. The world's oldest railway. Small collection of historic locos carrying steam hauled passenger services (Easter–Sept.)

Craft Centres and Art Galleries

Cartwright Hall, Bradford. The City's art gallery set in Lister Park. Tel. (0274) 493313

Leeds Central Art Gallery. Tel. (0532) 462495

Temple Newsam House. Tel. (0532) 647321

1853 Gallery, Salts Mill, Saltaire. Houses works by local-born David Hockney. Tel. (0274) 531163

Huddersfield Art Gallery. Tel. (0484) 513808

Leisure Centres and Swimming Pools

Richard Dunn Sports Centre, Odsal. Tel. (0274) 307872

Keighley Leisure Centre, Victoria Park. Tel. (0535) 602401

Nabwood Sports Centre, Bingley. Tel. (0274) 567285

Bradford Ice Rink, Little Horton Road. Tel. (0274) 733535

Halifax Pool. Tel. (0422) 66624

Leeds Olympic Pool. Tel. (0532) 438696

Kirkstall Leisure Centre. Tel. (0532) 786878

OTHER PLACES OF INTEREST

Shipley Glen Tramway. Cable-hauled tramway up through woodland to a small childrens' fairground. Tel. (0274) 685532.

Saltaire model village founded by industrialist Sir Titus Salt. Interesting architecture. Rowing boats may be hired on the nearby river Aire.

5-Rise Locks on the Leeds to Liverpool canal, Bingley. Amazing canal engineering feat lifts narrow boats 60 vertical feet.

Castle Hill, Almondbury, Huddersfield. Hill top site of fortifications dating back to Neolithic times. Jubilee Tower and 80ft deep medieval well.

TOURIST INFORMATION

Bradford: Central library, Princes Way. Tel. (0274) 33081
Leeds: Central library, Calverley Street. Tel. (0532) 462453
Halifax: Piece Hall, Westgate. Tel. (0422) 68725
Haworth: 2/4 West Lane. Tel. (0535) 42329
Hebden Bridge: 1 Bridge Gate. Tel. (0422) 843831
Huddersfield: 3/5 Albion Street. Tel. (0484) 422133
Ilkley: The Library, Station Road. Tel. (0943) 602319
Wakefield: Town Hall. Tel. (0924) 70211
Holmfirth: Huddersfield Road. Tel. (0484) 4992
Wetherby: Council Offices, Westgate. Tel. (0937) 62706
Todmorden: Tel. (0706) 818181

VIEWPOINTS

Druid's Altar, Bingley. G.R. SE093400
Stoodley Pike, Langfield Common. G.R. SD974241
Woodhouse Crag, Ilkley Moor. G.R. SE095470
Beacon Hill, The Chevin. G.R. SE199442
Penistone Hill, Haworth. G.R. SE020370

OTHER USEFUL INFORMATION

Countryside Organisations

Nature Conservancy Council, Archbold House, Archbold Terrace, Newcastle-upon-Tyne, NE2 1EG. Tel. (091) 2816316

Yorkshire Wildlife Trust, 10 Toft Green, York, North Yorkshire, YO1 1JT. Tel. (0904) 59570

The Ramblers Association, 1–5 Wandsworth Road, London, SW8 2XX. Tel. (071) 5826878

Forestry Commision, 1a Grosvenor Terrace, York, YO3 7BD. Tel. (0904) 620221

Youth Hostels

Youth Hostel Association

Bradford. Tel. (0274) 567697
Haworth. Tel. (0535) 642234
Mankinholes. Tel. (0706) 812340

Market Days

Halifax (Piece Hall)	Fri, Sat.
Bingley	Wed, Fri.
Leeds	Tues, Fri, Sat.
Huddersfield	Mon, Thurs.
Shipley	Fri, Sat.
Hebden Bridge	Thurs.
Todmorden	Wed, Fri, Sat.

PERSONAL SAFETY ON THE HILLS

It cannot be stressed enough that ramblers should go prepared for all eventualities. Pennine weather can change suddenly and be a complete contrast between the valleys and high fellsides. If crossing exposed moorland or high ground always:

Wear stout footwear and carry suitable waterproof.
Carry map and compass and have the knowledge to use them.
Carry a torch, whistle and spare food.
Leave details of your route and never walk alone.
Take extra caution with children near deep water.

In the event of an emergency never leave an injured person alone. If injuries allow it, move to a sheltered position safe from additional hazards, water, loose boulders or cliff edge. If unconscious leave in a position where vomiting is unlikely to cause choking.

Cover the injured party with spare clothing, or better still, place in an exposure bag. Remember the universally recognized distress signal is six long blasts on a whistle or flashes with a lamp, repeated at one minute intervals.

To summon help dial 999 and ask for Fell Rescue.

FAMILY WALKS SERIES

Family Walks in the Lake District. Barry McKay. ISBN 0 907758 40 1.
Family Walks in West Yorkshire. Howard Beck. ISBN 0 907758 43 6.
Family Walks in Three Peaks and Malham. Howard Beck. ISBN 0 907758 42 8.
Family Walks in South Yorkshire. Norman Taylor. ISBN 0 907758 25 8.
Family Walks in Cheshire. Chris Buckland. ISBN 0 907758 29 0.
Family Walks in the Staffordshire Peak and Potters. Les Lumsdon. ISBN 0 907758 34 7.
Family Walks in the White Peak. Norman Taylor. ISBN 0 907758 09 6.
Family Walks in the Dark Peak. Norman Taylor. ISBN 0 907758 16 9.
Family Walks in Snowdonia. Laurence Main. ISBN 0 907758 32 0.
Family Walks in Mid Wales. Laurence Main. ISBN 0 907758 27 4.
Family Walks in South Shropshire. Marian Newton. ISBN 0 907758 30 4.
Family Walks in the Teme Valley. Camilla Harrison. ISBN 0 907758 45 2.
Family Walks in Hereford and Worcester. Gordon Ottewell. ISBN 0 907758 20 7.
Family Walks in the Wye Valley. Heather and Jon Hurley. ISBN 0 907758 26 6.
Family Walks in the Cotswolds. Gordon Ottewell. ISBN 0 907758 15 0.
Family Walks in South Gloucestershire. Gordon Ottewell. ISBN 0 907758 33 9.
Family Walks in Oxfordshire. Laurence Main. ISBN 0 907758 38 X.
Family Walks around Bristol, Bath and the Mendips. Nigel Vile. ISBN 0 907758 19 3.
Family Walks in Wiltshire. Nigel Vile. ISBN 0 907758 21 5.
Family Walks in Berkshire and North Hampshire. Kathy Sharp. ISBN 0 907758 37 1
Family Walks on Exmoor and the Quantocks. John Caswell. ISBN 0 907758 46 0.
Family Walks in Mendip, Avalon and Sedgemoor. Nigel Vile. ISBN 0 907758 41 X.
Family Walks in North West Kent. Clive Cutter. ISBN 0 907758 36 3.

Ready Spring 1992

Family Walks in the Weald of Kent and Sussex
Family Walks in North Yorkshire
Family Walks around Luton and Dunstable
Family Walks in Northumbria
Family Walks in Nottinghamshire
Family Walks on the Isle of Wight
Family Walks in Clwyd
Family Walks in Dorset
Family Walks in Rossendale, Pendle and Bowland

Other titles under consideration

The Publishers, D. J. Mitchell and E. G. Power welcome suggestions for further titles in this Series; and will be pleased to consider other manuscripts of Derbyshire and regional interest from new or established authors.
